New England
Worships

100 Drawings of Churches and Temples

with accompanying text

by John Wedda

To Elspeth

First Printing

© Copyright, 1965, by John Wedda

All rights reserved under International and Pan-American Copyright
Conventions. Published in New York by Random House, Inc., and
simultaneously in Toronto, Canada, by Random House of Canada Ltd.

Library of Congress Catalog Card Number: 65-21218

Manufactured in the United States of America

TABLE OF CONTENTS

Foreword

The pages of this book are a picture, in words and drawings, of the changing face of faith in New England—from the coming of the Europeans to the present. It is not an effort to proselyte for or to criticize any of the faiths represented. It does not include all of the faiths which worship in these states. There was no intent behind either the inclusion or omission of denominations.

Exposed as provincial, chauvinistic myths are some of the generally accepted national and regional clichés. Complete separation of church and state was not accomplished with the birth of the United States. The Colonies were formed as combination church-civil societies which gave a single denomination the controlling voice in civil and church affairs. These church-state units were not supplanted by exclusively civil government until the eighteen-hundreds.

The exception was the Colony of Rhode Island, which was founded by Roger Williams to provide freedom of religious worship. Williams' concept did provide a measure of separation of civil and ecclesiastical controls.

When Thomas Hooker founded Connecticut in 1639, it was the first time in history that a state was created by a written constitution with no restriction of suffrage to church members. Hooker believed that all of the people ought to take part directly or indirectly in the work of governing; that those who did not themselves hold office ought at least to vote. Despite this foundation, Connecticut existed for many years as a church-state structure.

In this study the stereotype image of New Englanders as Yankees descended from the Mayflower settlers vanishes before the revelation that New England's people are a true amalgam of the world's ethnic strains. For here are representatives of the huddled masses who flocked to America as the promised land, and here is seen the assimilation of all into what is still developing as the American man.

The various styles of architecture show the relationships between congregations and the buildings in which they worship. Buildings reflect the personalities of their congregations and congregations reflect the characters of their churches.

Fire, lightning and the execrable taste of the mid-Victorian era are exposed as the great destroyers of much Colonial architectural beauty. In many cases the destruction of fine old buildings was brought about by a desire to be architecturally "fashionable." And the fashion marks a low point in American architecture. Simple, beautifully proportioned buildings were replaced by ill-conceived, malproportioned, gewgaw-burdened exercises in unnecessary complexity.

The "demon rum" is demonstrated to have been on the side of good work in the construction of the old churches and meeting houses, the costs of which would have been greatly increased without the stimulation which warmed the bodies and spirits of the volunteer builders. Even as late as the eighteen-twenties, this "demon" played an important part in church-raising. Well after Lyman Beecher had introduced temperance (a euphemism for abstinence) to his congregation, a new meeting house was waiting to be raised but no work was being done. Then a keg of rum was brought from the nearby tavern, and a miraculous burst of energy accomplished the task. No mention is made in the church history of Reverend Beecher's reaction to his congregation's source of inspiration.

The austerity of the early Calvinists has been tempered. Metaphysical relationships with church and God have given way to a larger concern for the relationships of man to man and man to God, within the area of his own time.

It happened that in Massachusetts, after the Revolution, a widow who re-married without the approval of the church was tried by a council of five ministers. She was found guilty because her new husband was said to have used profane language. She was excommunicated from the church, which took her children from her and placed them in an orphanage. This action was entirely by a church, rather than by a civil court. Such church council trials were not uncommon, nor was the severity of their punishments.

It is unthinkable, in present-day New England, that pacific people like the Quakers should be hanged or have their ears lopped off for their beliefs. Or even that they should, men and women together, be stripped to the waist and publicly flogged by the hangman. But these things were done in the early colonial days. They were done by people who, only a few years earlier, had been the targets of persecution as heretics.

It is not so easy to say that there could be no repetition of the mass madness evinced by the witch-hunts of Salem and its environs. Not only were charges made on the flimsiest evidence, but there was a total lack of defense from the charges. Anyone who dared to speak in favor of a defendant made himself liable as the next victim of the insanity. Conviction resulted in death by hanging, death by burning, death by drowning or death by being pressed.

Even the harshness and severity of pioneer life cannot excuse the cruelties practiced in the name of religion, for there were too many protesters to mal-treatment and intolerance.

It is a lesson which should be constantly before us that fanatic zeal, for whatever cause, makes men insensitive to the rights of other men. The religious intolerance and exclusivity of the colonial and early national periods have been replaced by the broad acceptance and freedom of religious belief which Americans cherish. There are many examples in New England of close co-operation, mutual assistance and respect between the various faiths. In this atmosphere all faiths can feel more secure.

Early colonial religious practice was not an easy thing. Sunday worship was an all-day activity for the entire family. The New Englander endured five to six hours of two-session services without the comfort of heat in the churches—and the winters were bitterly cold. In the history of a Hartford church the author quotes from the diary of an early member that "on one occasion the communion bread was frozen pretty hard and rattled sadly onto the plate."

Not until the eighteen-hundreds were church stoves installed in the majority of the meeting houses. The more sophisticated city folk apparently felt the need for heat earlier than did their country cousins. The *Evening Post* of January 25, 1783, printed the following jingle after the installation of the first stove in Old South Church, Boston:

> *Extinct the sacred fire of love,*
> *Our zeal grown cold and dead,*
> *In the house of God we fix a stove*
> *To warm us in their stead.*

The Shakers, once so important a part of the New England community, have almost vanished. But their influence remains strong. They were the first experimental agriculturists and commercial seedsmen, who improved farming throughout the country. They were the first to introduce botanical medical practice to America. They sought wild field and woods plants and maintained "physician's gardens." From these crops they prepared extracts and medicines sold in this country and abroad. The list of Shaker inventions demonstrates the importance of Shakerism to the early national economy. The Shakers were fine educators, whose methods presaged recent developments in teaching. They preferred to let pupils learn at their own rate, free from competitive pressures. Music was freely used to make study more attractive. A geography lesson began with this song:

> *Will you please to attend, every scholar and friend,*
> *To a tune from the musical fountain,*
> *Which will link in a chain the location and name*
> *Of some of the principal mountains.*

Then followed in rhyme the names of the mountains of the eastern United States. Another such song named the rivers, and so on. The Shakers taught Shaker and non-Shaker children alike in public schools and in their own private schools.

When we come to the present we see physical statements of the changes which American growth has brought with an accelerating pace. There is no gainsaying the contemporaneity of the congregations whose new structures of worship are more a reflection of a world made by man than they are of a world made by God.

Some of these expressions may have been motivated, as many were which preceded them, by superficialities. More important, they are manifestations of man's struggle for expression of self within the framework of the time of his existence, and these expressions are accurate mirrorings of these times.

One structure, whose architect and congregation strove consciously to create a statement of harmony and unity, resembles nothing so much as the tail fins of a gigantic rocket, which, in its precipitous flight, seems to have left them behind as it thrust itself heavenward. Another church has a steeple which appears to be the rocket itself, not yet launched from its concrete pad.

While such effects are not the intent of the builders, they are not inappropriate—for what today better symbolizes man's efforts to thrust himself out of his earthly environment? Certainly, through their very creativity of form and substance, they express a combination of the human necessity for religion and self-expression. They reflect a clear image of the changing face of faith.

The pages which divide the book by states are decorated with pictorial sections of the stained-glass windows at St. Joseph's Church in Canaan, Connecticut. The pictures of the ark, the robe and dice, the cock and the burning bush are familiar to all. The other two are less well known. Explanations of these are translations by T. H. White from a Latin bestiary of the twelfth century.

The Unicorn and the Maiden: "He is a very small animal like a ked, excessively swift, with one horn in the middle of his forehead, and no hunter can catch him. But he can be trapped by the following stratagem: a virgin girl is led to where he lurks, and there she is sent off by herself into the wood. He soon leaps into her lap when he sees her, and embraces her, and hence he gets caught."

The Lioness and Her Cubs: "The third feature is this, that when a lioness gives birth to her cubs, she brings them forth dead and lays them up lifeless for three days—until their father, coming on the third day, breathes in their faces and makes them alive. Just so did the Father Omnipotent raise Our Lord Jesus Christ from the dead on the third day. Quoth Jacob: 'He shall sleep like a lion, and the lion's whelp shall be raised.' "

MASSACHUSETTS

Ense petit placidam sub libertate quietem

By the sword we seek peace, but peace only under liberty

First Parish in Plymouth

UNITARIAN

Church of the Pilgrimage

CONGREGATIONAL

Plymouth, Massachusetts

At the foot of Burial Hill the Pilgrims built their first church in 1638. For eighteen years they had worshiped in the Common House and on the lower floor of the "Fort," erected in 1622 on the crest of the hill.

These were the people who in Scrooby, England, in 1606, had covenanted to form a creedless church estate. They were known as "Separatists" because of their having denied allegiance to the Anglican Church. Persecuted as heretics, they fled in 1608 to Holland, where they stayed till 1620, when they sailed to become the Plymouth Colony which established English control in New England.

The schism which took place in 1801 has resulted in the presence of two churches at the place where the Pilgrims had originally built their church. The majority of the congregation having voted to become Unitarian, the minority seceded; thus both of these churches claim Pilgrim heritage.

The First Parish Church must be considered to be the legal continuation of the church founded by the Pilgrim Fathers. To justify their claim as the religious heirs of the founders they quote the words of their first pastor, John Robinson, in his farewell sermon to the Mayflower passengers: "The Lord hath more truth and light yet to break forth from out His Holy Word."

The Church of the Pilgrimage can be said to have inherited the religious mantle which, woven in Scrooby and Leyden, wrapped the founders' faith.

First Congregational Society

UNITARIAN

Salem, Massachusetts

The first gathering of a Congregational church in America took place on this site in 1629.

Roger Williams briefly held the position of teacher here in 1631. He returned to Salem to be installed as minister of this church in 1635. In this church Williams preached the liberal doctrines which roused the ire of the Puritans who, once they had achieved control of men, were not ready to grant any more freedom of religious belief than had their persecutors. From here Williams fled the Boston Magistrates to establish Rhode Island with religious liberty for all.

The year 1692 brought days of dark hysteria and mass madness to the religious community that was Salem. For seven months the witch hunts and trials and executions blighted the town. The minister, Nicholas Noyes, took an active part in the persecutions, which left little if any room for defense against charges—any person willing to defend the innocence of the accused was likely himself to be charged with witchcraft. The Witch House still stands close by the site of the church—a church which later erased from its record the excommunications of two of its members who had been executed: Rebecca Nourse, hanged as a witch, and Giles Corey, pressed to death. Not only Salem residents took part in the madness. They came from other areas to get in on the action and other communities were infected.

The virulence of the illness which itself bewitched Salem resulted in a weakening of the absolute rigidity which had heretofore characterized the Puritanical religious posture.

The Old Ship Church

UNITARIAN

Registered National Historic Landmark

Hingham, Massachusetts

Erected in 1681, this is the oldest church structure in the United States to have been used continuously for public worship. Samuel Lincoln, original American ancestor of Abraham Lincoln, worshiped here regularly. It is known as the "Ship Church." The roof structure employs the techniques used in the building of old wooden ship hulls. Compass rosettes adorn the ceilings of the bell tower and the pulpit sounding board.

The church history is rich in anecdotes which reflect its early background. Its Loyalist minister figures in two of these.

During the Revolution, a little before Thanksgiving, which it was feared would be celebrated without foreign foods and fruits such as raisins, several well-laden British ships were storm-blown onto the coast and captured, so the feast day lacked none of the gustatory refinements. The minister, in his Thanksgiving Day sermon, said: "Oh, Lord, who art the infinite Disposer of all things, who rulest the winds and the waves according to thy own pleasure, we devoutly thank thee for the gracious interposition of thy Providence in wafting upon our shores so many of the rich bounties, to make glad the dwellings of thy people on this joyful occasion."

The same minister having suffered thefts of hay from his barn, lay in wait one dark night for the thief. The man, carrying a large load of stolen hay on his back, passed the concealed minister, who quietly ignited the hay from the rear. When the hay began to blaze the thief fled in consternation. Soon after, he came to the minister and confessed his thievery saying that the Almighty had sent fire from heaven to illuminate his guilt. This misimpression was not corrected by the clergyman.

The West Parish Church

CONGREGATIONAL

West Barnstable, Massachusetts

On a day in 1616, in the Borough of Southwark, across London Bridge from the old City of London, a group of men gathered to fast and pray. They wrote:

Joyning togeather they joyned both hands each with other Brother and stood in a ring-wise: their intent being declared, Henry Jacob and each of the Rest made some confession or profession of their Faith & Repentance (some were longer, some were briefer). Then they Covenanted togeather to walk in all God's Ways as he had revealed or should make known to them.

Henry Jacob, who had long been active as a Separatist, was named pastor of the newly gathered congregation. He had been jailed for a year by the Bishop of London but had lost none of his zeal for separatism from the Anglican Church.

In 1608 he had joined John Robinson in Leyden. His return to England resulted in the gathering of the Southwark church which, like Jacob, was more temperate in its position than were other dissidents of the time. Because they did not totally repudiate the Anglican Church, these people were criticized by both Separatists and Anglicans.

It was Henry Jacob who coined the name "Congregational" for the new faith, and his was the first church to be so called. Today, the congregation in Barnstable claims to be the first Congregational church to have been created.

It had been Henry Jacob's intent that his church should remain in England, but this was not to be. On April 29, 1632, John Lothrop (Jacob's successor as pastor) and the other members of the church were meeting secretly for worship in the home of Humphrey Barnet. Officers of the King surrounded the house and arrested the entire congregation, which was then imprisoned. In the summer of 1634, upon intercession of the Bishop of Lambeth, King Charles released Lothrop on condition that he be banished from England. September of the same year saw the arrival of Lothrop and thirty members of the Southwark church at Boston. They settled at Barnstable and maintained the church that exists today.

Old South Meeting House

Boston, Massachusetts

So long as Boston shall Boston be
And by her bay-tides rise and fall,
Shall freedom stand in the Old South Church
And plead for the rights of all.

—Whittier

Old South was the third Congregational church gathered in Boston. It originated in bitter contentions relating to the suffrage of non-church members of the Colony. South Church was organized as a protest against exclusivity, religious and political. In its very creation it stood for freedom of worship and political equality. It stood with the contentions of Thomas Hooker, the founder of Connecticut, that all men should have a voice in their government.

In 1687 Sir Edmund Andros, the oppressive governor, usurped the use of the church for Episcopal services, discommoding the regular members until 1689, when Andros was deposed.

Samuel Willard, the pastor of Old South, was regarded as a champion defending the cause of truth. In the witchcraft madness of 1692, though three of the judges who condemned persons executed for that "crime" were members of his church, Willard had the courage to publicly express disapproval of the measures pursued, to use his influence to stop them, and to aid some of the imprisoned accused to escape from the Colony.

In Old South it was voted to establish the first public school.

In 1767 began a series of meetings held at Old South which protested British actions: 1768, protest against impressment of sailors; 1770, demand for removal of King's regiments; 1773, Boston Tea Party meeting. Here Boston was roused to revolution.

Christ Church (Old North)

EPISCOPAL

Boston, Massachusetts

This must be the most famous steeple in American history. From its upper windows shone the lanterns which signaled the message carried by Paul Revere to Lexington. They lighted the start of the fight for independence.

It is the oldest existing church edifice in Boston and the second Anglican parish in the city.

The first rector was Timothy Cutler who, in 1722, as president of Yale College, shook New England Congregationalism by leaving that denomination for the Church of England. In England for his ordination, Cutler was honored by being given doctor's degrees from both Oxford and Cambridge. He was the first American to receive degrees from both these universities.

Cutler attracted to his church people of many religious faiths which were not viewed favorably by the Puritan community and had no churches of their own.

Patriots and Loyalists worshiped together in Christ Church. At one end of the left aisle is the pew of Robert Newman, who is believed to have hung the lanterns for Paul Revere. At the other end of the same aisle is the pew of Gen. Thomas Gage, the British commander of the siege of Boston. The rector of 1775, a Tory, fled to Nova Scotia.

Beneath the church is the crypt in which eleven hundred persons are buried. Among these is Maj. John Pitcairn, who led the British at Lexington and Concord. He was killed in the Battle of Bunker Hill. Years later, Westminster Abbey requested his body for interment there. It has been established that the wrong body was sent to England and that Pitcairn still rests in Christ Church crypt.

On the evening of each April 18th, a descendant of either Paul Revere or Robert Newman carries two lanterns into the steeple and gives the signal for neighborhood parades to begin.

First Parish Church

UNITARIAN

Lexington, Massachusetts

On this common was written the first bloody page of the Revolution. Paul Revere had alerted the Minutemen to the imminent arrival of the British troops marching from Boston. The Colonists faced the British from the far end of the common. Their leader, Capt. John Parker, told them: "Stand your ground. Don't fire unless fired upon! But if they mean to have a war, let it begin here!" The British officer commanded them to throw down their arms. Some began to disperse. A shot was fired. By whom? No one knows. No command to fire was given on either side. It sounded like a pistol shot fired from the sidelines at the British, who replied with a volley. The "battle" was of short duration but violent. It was the beginning of the War of Independence.

The present parsonage was then the home of Jonathan Harrington who, wounded on the common, dragged himself to the door and died at his wife's feet. Here, too, lived John Augustus, shoemaker, friend of the poor victims of the law, a pioneer in probation. Augustus devoted his time and means to the rehabilitation of convicted men given into his custody. He originated the idea of help for rather than jailing of wrongdoers.

A member of the church was Theodore Parker, grandson of the Minuteman captain, and contemporary of John Augustus. He was a man who filled the largest halls in Boston when he preached but was forbidden to appear in any pulpit and was vilified by his fellow ministers. He spoke eloquently all over the land for the human rights of the Negro. It was he who first used the phrase "a government of the people, by the people, for the people."

The Meeting-House of the First Parish

in Concord, Massachusetts

UNITARIAN UNIVERSALIST

Concord was the storehouse of the Minutemen's powder and supplies. At Concord Bridge was fired the "shot heard round the world" which resulted in the first defeat of the British. At the bridge are buried some of the British soldiers who fell there. At the other end of the bridge stands the statue of a Minuteman on the spot from which the shot was fired.

In the meeting house of the first parish the Provincial Congress met on the eve of the Revolution while the committees met in Wright's Tavern, immediately adjacent. The tavern was headquarters for the Minutemen in the early hours of April 19, 1775. Later that day it was the HQ of the British under Col. Smith and Major John Pitcairn.

The tavern is now owned by the Parish Corporation. The second floor houses Walden Clinic, a child guidance and psychiatric center whose name is reflective of the seeking of self and personal peace which nearby Walden Pond represented to Thoreau.

Ralph Waldo Emerson, the "Sage of Concord," was a member of the parish but not of the church. The duality of controlling societies is still maintained here. Parish membership was necessary for suffrage and the parish, maintained by public taxation, governed the physical properties and called the minister, who was paid from public tax moneys. The Church Society, whose membership was open only to communicants of the church, governed religious affairs. This is a hangover from the old church-state association, which maintained governmental control of the community.

A few years ago, the people of Concord contributed money for the restoration of All Saints' Episcopal Church in Odell, Bedfordshire, England. This was the church whose pastor, Peter Bulkeley, in 1635 became a Puritan, came to America and founded Concord.

King's Chapel

UNITARIAN

Registered National Historic Landmark

Boston, Massachusetts

Two firsts are the claim of King's Chapel. It was the first permanently established Anglican church in New England and the first avowed Unitarian church in America.

In 1686, the Rev. Robert Radcliffe landed in Boston with a commission from the King to found an Anglican church in that city. It was built in the public burying ground where colonial and state governors lie at rest.

The triple-tiered pulpit, installed in 1718, is the oldest in the United States in continuous use in its original site.

The present building, erected in 1749, is the first large public building built of granite. The organ is said to have been selected by Handel.

For its protection during the Revolution, King's Chapel was called simply The Stone Chapel.

The Rev. James Freeman, known widely as a Unitarian, having twice been refused ordination from Episcopal hands, was ordained according to congregational usage by the members of King's Chapel in 1787. The church thus became the first avowedly Unitarian church in America.

Today, King's Chapel maintains its full strength as a parish, still located on its first site near the original Free School.

St. Michael's Church

EPISCOPAL

Marblehead, Massachusetts

This is the oldest Episcopal church building in continuous use in New England. It was built in 1714, seven years after Episcopal services began in Marblehead. Here the non-conformists who had been exiled from England by the Anglican Church had become the established Church and the Anglicans were the non-conformists.

The English Colonies were established by various religious groups, each of which was anxious to retain its own domain. The Virginia Colony was as rigid in its establishment of the Anglican Church as the Massachusetts Colony was in its Puritanism. Not until the arrival of an oppressive representative of the King in 1686 was the Anglican Church able to establish itself with any success in New England.

As did other churches, St. Michael's suffered the loss of its Tory rector during the Revolution. His staunch loyalty to the Crown necessitated a sudden departure for Nova Scotia and England.

Many Anglican churches suffered damage at the hands of the patriots, who resented Anglican loyalty to the Crown. On learning of the signing of the Declaration of Independence, the townspeople of Marblehead rang the bell of St. Michael's till it was cracked. It was Paul Revere who later recast it.

At one point in its history St. Michael's was almost taken over by a group of Congregationalists who had first broken away from the First Parish Church and later separated from the second Congregational church when it voted to adopt Unitarianism. The dissident group bought a sufficient number of pews to gain control of St. Michael's, but the courts decided that the moneys contributed to the construction and maintenance of the church had been given with the intent and expectation that it would remain Anglican. It has.

The First Church of Deerfield

UNITED

Old Deerfield, Massachusetts

Registered National Historic Landmark

The history of Deerfield and its church is a saga of pioneer perseverance over an inhospitable land and Indian savagery. The massacre at Bloody Brook in 1675, by King Philip's warriors, wiped out the flower of Deerfield's youth. From time to time settlers were abducted and carried to Canada.

By 1696, the third meeting house had been erected, within the stockaded area of the village. Today, its replica stands next to the Brick Church and serves as the post office.

In 1704, incited by the French, Indians attacked the settlement. They swept quietly over the frozen snow to the drifts at the stockade walls. The sleeping sentry and the high drifts made it easy to gain access to the enclosure, many of whose buildings were burned. Forty-seven of the settlers were massacred and 112 were taken captive. These captives, including Rev. John Williams and those members of his family who had survived, were marched to Canada. Twenty more died or were killed on this trip, one of whom was Reverend Williams' pregnant wife. Williams was redeemed from captivity in 1706 and continued his service to Deerfield till his death in 1729.

The church bell was taken by the Indians. The Legend of the Bell of St. Regis claims that this bell was the real cause of the massacre. A French ship, carrying the bell to Canadian Indians, was captured by the British and its cargo sold at auction at Salem. The bell was bought for the church at Deerfield and installed. This incident was reputedly used by the French to incite the Indians to violence.

Despite the repeated setbacks which resulted from Indian incursions, Deerfield persisted and prospered in the paths of liberty. The pioneer spirit remains in a Deerfield so successfully restored to its colonial character that the town is now a Registered National Historic Landmark.

Park Street Church,

on the Boston Common

CONGREGATIONAL

Park Street Church was founded in 1809 by an ecclesiastical council formed to compensate for the Unitarian landslide which had claimed 15 of 17 Boston churches. Two ministers in the council were the fathers of two famous Americans, S. F. B. Morse and poet-author Oliver Wendell Holmes.

Built on the site of the town granary where the sails for the frigate *Constitution* were made, Park Street Church is considered one of the finest historical and patriotic shrines of early America.

Powder for use in the War of 1812 was stored in the church crypt, which was henceforth known as "Brimstone Corner."

In the vestry of this church an 1819 meeting was held which constituted the Sandwich Island (Hawaiian) Church.

From this pulpit William Lloyd Garrison delivered his first public address against slavery. In this church, exactly three years later, on the Fourth of July, 1832, "America" was sung for the first time.

Park Street Church is the third stop on the Freedom Trail, a tour through the historic shrines of old Boston.

First Parish Church

UNITARIAN

Lancaster, Massachusetts

Lancaster boasts one of the churches designed by Charles Bullfinch, architect of the Capitol, designer of Boston's Faneuil Hall, the Boston State House, the Boston Theater, court houses, hospitals, asylums, prisons, banks, schools, and entire streets of residences.

On Benjamin Henry Latrobe's resignation from service as the government architect in Washington, Bullfinch applied for the position, through John Quincy Adams, and was appointed at an annual salary of $2,500. Bullfinch completed the early work on the Capitol. He is one of the important figures of American Colonial and post-Colonial Architecture.

In her early days in America, Mother Ann Lee came to Lancaster and gathered a substantial following for her Shaker movement, a following which established three Shaker communities in that area.

Many of those who joined the Shakers were members of the First Parish Church, which voted not to censure, punish or excommunicate the "defectors" since it was felt that they could not have been of sound mind to have taken such a step.

A demonstration of the wry humor retained by even the strict Calvinists can be found in a story concerning the father of Ralph Waldo Emerson. Reverend Emerson was in the habit of going into the most minute particulars of thanks when saying grace. As a dinner guest in Lancaster, in a prolonged listing of the items of food on the table, he failed to mention a small plate of pickerel. His host, with a twinkle in his eye, said: "Very pretty little fish, but hardly worth praying about."

Seamen's Bethel

INTERDENOMINATIONAL

Johnnycake Hill, New Bedford, Massachusetts

Lat 41°38'08" N
Long 70°55'26" W

In the same New Bedford there stands a Whaleman's Chapel, and few are the moody fishermen, shortly bound for the Indian or Pacific Oceans, who failed to make a Sunday visit to this spot.

Moby Dick by Herman Melville

The Seamen's Bethel was built and dedicated in 1832 for the moral and spiritual improvement of the sailors who manned the whaling ships that called New Bedford their home port.

For many years the work of the Bethel was carried on by voluntary contributions which were percentages of the revenues of whaling voyages.

The walls of the chapel are lined with twenty-three cenotaphs. Some are memorials to individual men, some to two or three men, some to entire crews. The youngest of these was eighteen years old, the oldest only forty-nine. Most were in their early twenties. The earliest loss so memorialized occurred in 1818, the most recent was the loss of the lightship *Nantucket* in 1934.

The vestry of the Bethel is known as "The Old Salt Box" for two reasons: because it is symbolic of the hold of the ship, directly below the deck, in which fish was preserved in salt in the absence of ice; and because the redemptive work of the chapel is equated with the preservative function of the salt. A late chaplain wrote these lines:

"The Old Salt Box"—so named of yore
By whalers blunt on trips ashore—
The Bethel vestry, where they came
When lays were good and wealth and fame
Were theirs; or when, by woes beset,
They sought to restfully forget;
"The Old Salt Box"—preserving place
For men redeemed of every race.

First Congregational Church

Stockbridge, Massachusetts

The charter members of this historic church were Mohican Indians who, in 1734, ceded some land to the Massachusetts Colony. Their chief, Captain Konkapot, so impressed Rev. Dr. Samuel Hopkins that he arranged for a committee to meet with the Indians to propose that a Christian mission be established to instruct them in Christianity and to teach their children to read and write.

After four days of deliberation the Indians voted to invite a minister to come to the area. A church was organized on October 29, 1734, and a house of worship was dedicated Thanksgiving Day, November 29, 1739. John Sergeant was the first minister and during his tenure about 180 were baptized and Captain Konkapot and Lieutenant Umpachene were received into church membership. Under the tutelage of Reverend Sergeant the Indians flourished.

The Mohican Indians have long since left Stockbridge, having moved first to land in New York given them by the Oneidas, land which they named New Stockbridge. But they were not content there, and moved again, this time to settle in Gresham, Wisconsin. In Red Springs, Wisconsin, they established the Sergeant Memorial Church. The First Congregational Church of Stockbridge is still regarded by the "Stockbridge Indians" as their mother church, established by and for the Indians as "the pillar and ground of truth," a place for rest, recreation and worship of God. "God," they say, "is a Spirit and they that worship Him must worship in spirit and truth."

When the Indians' new church was dedicated they were given a new Communion service. In recognition of this gift, the Indians presented the Stockbridge Church with part of the original Communion service which they had taken with them when they left New England.

Old Parish Church

CONGREGATIONAL

Sheffield, Massachusetts

In June of 1733 the inhabitants of Sheffield, the first village of the Berkshires, were directed to build, within the space of three years, a suitable meeting house for the "publick" worship of God. These good people anticipated that directive by five months, having already voted to build such a structure. "Twenty gallons of rhumb [rum] and twenty pounds of sugar to go with the rhumb" were voted by the town to spur the workers.

The year 1760 saw the building of a new meeting house, which still graces the town green. In 1761 Col. John Ashley was appointed to designate the pews in the new meeting house. This was done by assigning the pews according to "dignatie," a custom dropped in the next ten years when widows and elderly people were given consideration in seating and boys and girls were seated on opposite sides of the gallery.

Two members of the congregation figured in one of the first legal freeings of a slave in our country. Mombette, a female slave owned by Colonel Ashley, ran away and asked the Sheffield attorney, Mr. Sedgwick, for help. Sedgwick gave her sanctuary, resisted Ashley's efforts to reclaim Mombette, and instituted legal proceedings on her behalf. Sedgwick pleaded for Mombette's freedom on the basis of the law that all men were created equal. He won the case and the grateful Mombette spent the remainder of her life with the Sedgwicks. On her death she was buried in the Sedgwick family plot in the burying ground at Stockbridge.

The First Church of Templeton

UNITED

Templeton, Massachusetts

This church has an unusual denominational history. In 1753 its first meeting house was built, and in 1755 the church was organized, with no denominational creed but with a covenant signed by the twelve founders. The official church of the Colony being the Congregational, this denomination was adopted for a short time till it was superseded here by the Unitarian Congregational Society.

Until 1832 the church served both Unitarian and Congregational members. It was then that the Congregationalist members, feeling the need for Trinitarian worship, built their own church, assisted by their Unitarian brethren.

The year 1939 saw a rejoining of the two groups in a federated church of Unitarian and Trinitarian Congregationalists, with each group keeping affiliation with its national parent body.

In 1956 a Special Act of the state legislature made possible the formation of the First Church of Templeton, which truly united the congregation in one church organization.

To eliminate any possibility of divided loyalties, the Trinitarian Congregational Church built in 1832 was razed by its former users when they rejoined the First Church.

The United Church of New Marlboro

CHRIST CONGREGATIONAL

New Marlboro, Massachusetts

Tucked away in the backwoods of the Berkshire Hills of Massachusetts is the township of New Marlboro, which is made up of five small villages, each with its own churches. Three of these were independent Congregational churches which served their respective communities separately until 1960, when they were united under one constitution as the United Church of New Marlboro.

Because each village revered its church, all three are being maintained and used in alternate seasons. Worship is conducted at Mill River from September to December and from May to June; at New Marlboro during July and August; and at Southfield from December to May.

The seasonal assignments were determined by the heating systems of the respective churches. Mill River's heat is adequate for autumn and spring requirements. Southfield's system is sufficient to withstand winter's cold. New Marlboro needs no heat in the summer months.

Near the New Marlboro church is a small stone monument to Elihu Burritt, the "learned blacksmith," who taught himself fifty languages. The monument is topped by Burritt's anvil. He was an apostle of peace who took his message around this country and abroad. He organized the League of Universal Brotherhood, successfully advocated low-rate ocean postage and, as the author of *The Congress of Nations*, presaged the League of Nations and the United Nations. Because of his lowly status as blacksmith, Burritt's plea for the hand of a New Marlboro girl was spurned by her father. Thereafter Burritt went on to world travel and fame.

The United Church of New Marlboro

CHRIST CONGREGATIONAL

Mill River, Massachusetts

The Mill River member of the tri-church union of New Marlboro looks out over the village from its place of eminence, proudly displaying its beautiful steeple—bright in daylight and brighter by floodlight. The first indication that a traveler is nearing a village is the sight of the thin, distant spire rising above the treetops.

All seasons of the year are beautified by the clean whiteness of this Colonial-Victorian building. The brilliant autumn colors of foliage still clinging or already shed, the gray of clouded, damp sky, and the mossy green of hospitable rock are all heightened by contrast with the dramatic simplicity of clean clapboard and plank.

The rural quietness of the township is in strange contrast to the purpose for which New Marlboro was originally chartered. It, along with neighboring townships, was created to insure protection and maintenance of "the great road" between Westfield and Sheffield, part of a colonial road planned to link Boston with Albany. A once important thoroughfare, this road now serves primarily as a link for the towns it brought into being.

The United Church of New Marlboro

CHRIST CONGREGATIONAL

Southfield, Massachusetts

The lovely lines of Southfield Church are a happy blending of Colonial and Greek Revival classicism.

Inside its doors is displayed a scroll written in a hand very similar to that in which the Declaration of Independence was penned. But the words of this scroll might more accurately be described as a "declaration of interdependence":

The Congregational Churches of New Marlboro—First Church (1744), Southfield (1794) and Mill River (1873)—wishing to be of greater strength and more effective witness to Jesus Christ among their brethren, have joined together in worship, in the education of their youth, in supporting a minister, and as of 1957, in operating under the same budget. In the year 1960, with the historical difficulty of distance removed by the automobile, with the population of the Township and our individual churches reduced, and with an experienced oneness of mind and concern, the Congregational Churches of New Marlboro do undertake to become the United Church of New Marlboro. This union, we trust, is called for by God that we may be stronger in our fellowship and more effective in our witness among men. To that end in dependence upon God we do dedicate ourselves.

Saint Luke's Church

EPISCOPAL

Lanesboro, Massachusetts

The sounds of psalm, prayer and hymnal no longer reverberate within the age-bulged walls of this beautiful Gothic stone structure. The dwindling congregation is now served by the small frame parish house in the village.

St. Luke's parish was organized in 1767, and in 1768 the congregation's first church building was erected. It is not strange that the first rector of this Church of England house of worship should have had Tory sympathies—sympathies not shared by his flock of faithful revolutionaries. Paradoxically, the church is said to have benefited in a remarkable way from the Revolution.

Hessian soldiers, encamped in a Lanesboro meadow, refused to pay the owner for the use of the land. While the mercenaries were in a drunken stupor at night, their paymaster's money disappeared. One of the townsfolk, who afterward displayed a sudden affluence, became one of the major early benefactors of the church.

The stone church was opened on Christmas Day of 1836, and through its years of service, the congregation seemed to have been guided by the spirit of the painter, St. Luke, in beautifying the walls with frescoes and the windows with stained glass.

Now the economic changes which have drawn the young from simple village life have apparently doomed this lovely edifice to the quiet decay of disuse.

Our Lady of Good Voyage

ROMAN CATHOLIC

Gloucester, Massachusetts

Many of the Portuguese fishermen who came to Gloucester from the Azores did not come as immigrants. The Portuguese government of the time would not allow emigration. The fishermen were supposed to return to their Portuguese homes after five years. Wives and families were kept under Portuguese authority to insure the return of the fishermen after they had completed the prescribed time. Many did return, but there were many who found the pull of the new land stronger than family ties. Some of these who wished to marry and found families here caused serious problems for the Church, which could not sanction such action.

It is a tribute to the piety of these people that they suffered no diminution of loyalty to the Catholic Church, though for many years they were without a church of their own.

The statue of Our Lady of Good Voyage faces the sea from a high position between the twin blue towers of the church. In her left arm she cradles a full-rigged schooner. Her right hand is raised to the harbor in blessing. When a fishing vessel is due to make port at night, the Captain radiophones ahead and the statue is illuminated, to stand as a beacon for the safety of the harbor.

One Sunday each year the schooners and draggers blossom out in pennants and pass in procession to receive the blessing of the Bishop or the Cardinal. Annually, too, there is the memorial service when girls in white frocks cast garlands on the waters, wreaths taken out to sea by the evening ebb tide to commemorate the lost fishermen of Gloucester.

Church of Saint John in the Wilderness

EPISCOPAL

Taconic State Park

Copake Falls, New York

Here is a natural setting for a natural building. Woods, hills, mountains and sky are its companions. There is nothing dramatic, imposing or arresting about it—only a quiet harmony between man's structure and God's nature.

Silver-gray board and batten walls, simple, open steeple, high pitch roof, weathered brick of chimney, combine to form an unpretentious serenity with self and surroundings. From its hilltop, Saint John's issues a quiet invitation to share contemplative communion with nature.

The interior of this 112-year-old church achieves its own harmony of simple, almost rustic, Gothic beams and age-stained plaster walls softly lit in the daylight hours by colored light transmitted through stained-glass windows, and at night by the flickering light of two hundred candles. Even in the outside entry the use of electric illumination is eschewed.

This is a place for contemplation and reunion with personal peace, uncrowded and unhurried. Its situation in a state park should insure that it will remain such a place indefinitely.

For many years the exact location of the line separating New York from Massachusetts in this area was in contention. Final resolution of the question placed Saint John's in New York. It is hoped that New York will not resent the inclusion of this church in a book of New England worship.

The Mother Church

THE FIRST CHURCH OF CHRIST, SCIENTIST

Boston, Massachusetts

The Church of Christ, Scientist, was founded in 1879 when fifteen students of Mary Baker Eddy met with their teacher and voted to "organize a church designed to commemorate the word and works of our Master, which should reinstate primitive Christianity and its lost element of healing."

A few years later the church took its present form as the mother church, the First Church of Christ, Scientist, in Boston. Together with its branch churches and societies throughout the world, it constitutes the Christian Science denomination.

Mary Baker Eddy was born in Bow, New Hampshire, in 1821. In her early years she manifested deep spirituality. Early widowhood, protracted ill health and an enforced separation from her only child stimulated her desire to find a practical understanding of God. The result of her search was a belief that the origin of all disease is mental, but it was not until 1866—when she was healed of the effects of a serious accident as she pondered one of Jesus' healings—that she felt that the answer was revealed to her. Her own remarkable recovery led her to a devoted study of the Bible to discover the science of Christ's healings.

Mrs. Eddy established her church on principle rather than on human personality. Unlike many who founded, or on whose teachings were founded, religions, she is in no way deified or worshiped. Her own admonition was to "follow your leader only so far as she follows Christ."

Christian Science has no missionaries in the usual sense of the word. It has been spread largely through the examples of the lives of many of its followers and through the healings which are a part of their faith and worship.

Armenian Church of our Saviour

ARMENIAN APOSTOLIC

Worcester, Massachusetts

This is the first Armenian church to have been established in America. Its founding in 1890 preceded the main waves of Armenian emigration which followed the 1895 and post-World War I massacres and persecutions in Turkey.

Armenian history claims very early adoption of Christianity as its national faith—the years of acceptance having been during the missions of Sts. Thaddeus and Bartholomew.

In the year 301 A.D., Christianity was proclaimed the national religion of Armenia. Until that time a struggle had raged between Christians and "pagans," who were referred to as "fire-worshipers." Such reference causes conjecture as to whether the pagans were in fact Zoroastrians, who are neither pagans nor fire-worshipers. The sun and fire are used as religious symbols by the Zoroastrians, whose faith was actually a precursor of the Judaic and Christian beliefs.

As have been many other constantly dominated peoples, the Armenians are devoted to the maintenance of ethnic identity and individuality. Denial of political independence seems to inspire the most stubborn retention of ethnic character. None is stronger than that of the Armenians, which has successfully survived two thousand years of domination by Persia, Islam, Turkey and Russia.

The Church of Our Saviour is an example of Armenian tradition. It is built in the architectural form which has come down the corridors of time from the first Armenian cathedral, the Etchmiadzin, built near Mt. Ararat early in the fourth century.

St. Francis Xavier Church

ROMAN CATHOLIC

Hyannis, Massachusetts

Only one church has had altar boys who later became senators, attorney general and President. It is St. Francis Xavier, the church at which the Joseph Kennedy family has worshiped for many years.

The main altar is a memorial to Joseph P. Kennedy, Jr., who was killed August 12, 1944, while piloting a bomber on a secret mission to destroy a V-2 missile base. To commemorate the younger Kennedy's service as a naval aviator, the altar bears the insignia of the Navy and the Naval Aviation Service. Insignia of St. Joan and St. George honor two warrior saints; the latter commemorates the senior Kennedy's service as ambassador to England.

The second pew of the new chapel bears a plaque marking the seat habitually occupied by the late President John F. Kennedy. A small anteroom behind the sacristy housed the Secret Service men who waited by the closet that contained a telephone connected to the White House. Even while at Mass in Hyannis the President was only a few steps from the nerve center of the country.

That the possibility of his assassination had occurred to the President is demonstrated by a remark he once made in this church. At one service, the President looked over his shoulder and said to one of the correspondents sitting in the pew behind him: "You know, if someone wanted to take a shot at me, he would have to shoot through your hat."

Ramakrishna Vedanta Society

Boston, Massachusetts

Vedanta, often incorrectly equated with Hinduism, is the philosophy which has evolved from the teachings of the Vedas, the oldest religious writings in existence. Vedanta includes not only the Vedas themselves but the whole mass of literature which has developed from them. It is a philosophy which teaches that all men are representatives of one God and that all men are a divine part of God—in a true brotherhood. One may follow the Vedanta principles without giving up the religious faith to which he subscribes.

Vedanta says: "Every soul is your own soul. Every creature is yourself. If you harm anyone, you harm yourself. Therefore, all feelings of separateness, exclusiveness, intolerance, and hatred are not only wrong, they are the blackest ignorance, because they deny the existence of the omnipresent Godhead, which is one. Truth is universal."

Vedanta was brought to America by the Swami Vivekananda when he represented Hinduism at the 1893 World Parliament of Religions in Chicago. His success was so great that he was invited to remain and teach in the United States. This he did for three years, founding the first Vedanta Society in New York. But it was in and around Boston that the Swami first introduced Vedanta in America, several weeks before the Chicago Parliament. He was offered the Chair in Eastern Philosophy at Harvard, but refused it.

The present Swami is one of the religious counselors at MIT, conducting the Friday afternoon religious services in the MIT Chapel.

Temple Anshe Amunim

JUDAIC REFORMED

Pittsfield, Massachusetts

This ninety-five-year-old congregation dedicated its new temple in 1964 (5724). The previous temple was acquired in 1927, having first been an Adventist church. It was the congregation's first building of its own.

The award-winning architecture of Temple Anshe Amunim was executed to reflect the fundamental Jewish concept, which stresses the Unity and Oneness of God. Thus, the cantilevered block design incorporates the three fundamental congregational activities of education, social activity and worship into a single body situated on sloping terrain which is employed, from entryway to ark, to symbolize Moses' journey up Mt. Sinai to receive the Tablets of the Law. The huge boulders express the rocky character of the Mount. Inside the sanctuary, the circular dome permits a clear view of sky and trees to emphasize that nature is the creation of the Almighty.

The ark, visible from the street, incorporates into a single unit the Eternal Light, the Menorah and the Ten Commandments, which are cut through the doors and illuminated from behind so that they may be seen night and day as reminders of the Lord's Laws.

The cast stone exterior symbol, identifying the building as a Jewish house of worship, is made of fifth-century Hebrew characters spelling the words *Anshe Amunim*, which mean "People of Faith."

The immigrant founders of this congregation who worshiped so long without their own temple building should be gratified at this solid evidence that they were truly people of a faith which has borne rich fruit.

Chinese Christian Church of New England

INTERDENOMINATIONAL

Boston, Massachusetts

From the Orient, ships brought the treasures of the East to New England. Tea and spices for the palate, silks and laces for the body, pottery for the table, teak and mahogany for ships and homes, art for the collector, and people for lowly work.

The familial and ethnic closeness of the Chinese has combined with Occidental unreadiness to accept the exotic in human form to stand in the way of assimilation of the Chinese into the general community. As a result, many Chinese have been slow to learn the language and customs of their adopted country.

In 1947, a year after the organization of the Chinese Christian Church, another Chinese arrived in Boston—Dr. Peter Shih, former dean of the West China Union Theological Seminary. He takes pride in being called a "Chinese missionary to America."

Dr. Shih and his wife carry on a dual mission calculated to benefit both Occidental and Chinese Americans. A major purpose of the church is the education of the adult Chinese, teaching them English and aiding them to gain American citizenship.

The second aim is the sharing of Chinese culture with Americans through lectures, dinner parties, celebrations, and radio and television programs. Each year the church puts on a Chinese New Year program at John Hancock Hall, attended by hundreds of non-Chinese.

It is a completely interdenominational, interracial work which encourages full interchange of ideas and experiences.

St. James the Fisherman

EPISCOPAL

Wellfleet, Massachusetts

Cape Codders are proud of their churches, most of which are small and intimate structures whose congregations swell and shrink with the seasons.

The "summer people" are as devoted to the Cape as are the year-round residents and feel as strong a debt as they do to the hospitality of this thin spit of land that curves out into the sea from Plymouth.

Two such summer "Codders," a couple from Worcester, were primarily responsible for the creation of the summer chapel called St. James the Fisherman. They and the architect, another summer resident of the Cape, did not want to remain with traditional forms, but neither did they want to build something that would be out of place in the Cape setting of scrub pine and sandy soil. What resulted is a structure that weds itself to its surroundings most harmoniously.

This is a "church-in-the-round," designed in an essentially square exterior structure. The eight major beams rise from the floor around the centrally located altar to form the structural heart of the steeple. Daylight is taken in through the plastic bubble over the altar. This concentration of light provides drama to the focal point toward which the entire design is directed. The five banks of seats have been so arranged that none of the three hundred and twenty worshipers is more than six rows from the altar.

Stones from Truro Cathedral, the Colosseum and the Parthenon are set into the thresholds of the three doors.

Mount Toby Meeting

SOCIETY OF FRIENDS

Leverett, Massachusetts

And so I find it well to come
For deeper rest to this still room,
For here the habit of the soul
Feels less the outer world's control;
The strength of mutual purpose pleads
More earnestly our common needs;
And from the silence multiplied
By these still forms on either side,
The world that time and sense have known
Falls off and leaves us God alone.
—John Greenleaf Whittier

This new meeting house is the first building to house the Mt. Toby Quakers, an amalgamation of four former meetings of the area. Because there were not enough children in the individual meetings to justify four Sunday schools, the Mt. Toby group was formed to provide full facilities for the young as well as the adult Quakers.

A substantial portion of the building is devoted to the operation of the meeting's clothing program, which gathers, repairs, cleans and distributes clothing through the American Friends Service Committee to all parts of the world where aid is needed.

The entire membership was involved in the planning of every aspect of the building and its furnishings. Benches, which are arranged circularly around the meeting room, were designed and redesigned, finished and refinished until complete harmony was accomplished to provide a room ideally suited to peaceful contemplation.

CONNECTICUT

Qui transtulit sustinet

He who transplanted still survives

The Sterling Divinity Quadrangle

NONDENOMINATIONAL

Yale University

The ministerial needs of southern New England, from the earliest days of the seventeen-hundreds, were filled by Yale University, whose founding fathers had committed themselves to the propagation of "the blessed reformed Protestant religion in this wilderness."

It was almost a self-perpetuating chain that developed, since the graduates who went forth as ministers became educators who not only influenced young minds from the pulpit but acted as preparators who readied young men for college. Students who had completed the undergraduate course received further training for the ministry in the homes of pastors who directed their studies and trained them in the practical as well as the theological aspects of the clergyman's work.

It was, in a sense, an oligarchic structure with a trinity of purpose: the perpetuation of a theology founded on intellectual enlightenment; an affirmation of pietism which stressed conscience, heart and emotional devotion; humanitarianism which manifested itself in social reform.

Yale was the one place which early practiced this trinity of purpose and maintained it in an unbroken continuity which has demonstrated a capability for growth to meet the changing requirements of a changing society.

The First Church of Christ

CONGREGATIONAL

Wethersfield, Connecticut

Wethersfield is one of the three oldest towns in Connecticut and the Congregational church is one of the oldest buildings in the state. It is known as the "Onion Church."

The cost of building a brick church of this size in 1761-64 was relatively high and the taxes levied to pay for the construction were deemed to be burdensome for an agricultural community. A town meeting voted "to accept, in lieu of money, the red onions grown and shipped from this place, at 3d per bunch [a rope], provided they were well cured."

The Old South Church of Boston served as a model for the architecture. Some of the materials used were salvaged from the previous meeting house, built in 1685, which was dismantled.

A new clock and a new bell, ordered in 1784, were paid for by a tax of "two and one quarter bunches of onions to the £ on the list of 1783." The clock was not installed in the steeple till the Ecclesiastical Society had satisfied itself that it was "fully equal to that in the Farmington Society Church." The bell, when brought from New Haven, was rung in each of the towns through which it passed.

The semicircular seating is another unusual feature of this fine old colonial meeting house.

First Church of Christ

CONGREGATIONAL

Farmington, Connecticut

"It deserves to be remembered also in the annals of this house that after these agitations [anti-slavery movement] had begun to subside, some forty Africans who had been set free by the authority of the nation, were regularly present in it for months, as an earnest of the great deliverance which was to follow a quarter of a century afterward. When these Africans became residents of this town, and every Lord's day appeared in this house of Christian worship, their presence was felt to hallow this place and gave emphasis to the oft repeated prayer, 'Thy Kingdom Come.'"

The above quotation is a footnote taken from the history of the Farmington Congregational church, written in 1871 on the occasion of the building's one hundredth anniversary. It is a modest allusion to an incident of the 1840's in which Farmington and the church played an important part. It is a story of liberation from slavery, begun in 1839 when the schooner *Amistad*, making a short island-to-island trip in the Caribbean, was the scene of a violent uprising by the cargo of slaves, who had been roused by threats that they were to be killed and eaten.

The slaves killed the ship's brutal captain but spared the lives of the two slave owners after they had promised to navigate the ship to Africa. These treacherous men violated their promise and sailed the ship coastwise to the north till it was apprehended off New London.

After exoneration by the New London court the thirty-seven Africans were offered sanctuary by the people of Farmington. Most were domiciled in a large dormitory-like building. The children and women were taken as guests into private homes. The Africans were Farmington's guests for two years, until 1842, when they were provided with transportation to Africa. Their erstwhile hosts provided equipment and funds to enable the Africans to establish new homes on their native continent. With the equipment and money, they established, near Sierra Leone, a mission which they called Mendi, after the place in Africa from which they had been abducted and taken into slavery. One of the thirty-seven did not live to see Africa again. He lies at rest in the old burying ground near the Farmington church.

First Ecclesiastical Society

UNITARIAN

Brooklyn, Connecticut

The spirit of independence asserted itself early in this area of Connecticut. In 1721 the people living within a portion of the towns of Canterbury and Pomfret petitioned the legislature to be set off as a separate Ecclesiastical Society. Ten years went by before the plea was granted. Then the people were determined to have a minister of their own choice despite the disapproval of the ecclesiastical authorities of Windham County. When the Ecclesiastical Court dismissed their junior minister, the Rev. Luther Willson, for heresy, the congregation forthwith sought Unitarian affiliation and called to the pulpit the Rev. Samuel J. May, whose sister, then living with him in Brooklyn, later became the wife of Bronson Alcott and the mother of Louisa May Alcott.

Gen. Israel Putnam became a member of the Society in 1747, and in 1760 decided that Brooklyn should have a new meeting house. This precipitated a head-on clash between Putnam and Colonel Godfrey Malbourne. The mutual antipathy of these two men toward each other resulted in a struggle which went on for ten years before a town vote settled the issue in favor of Putnam's position.

Malbourne retaliated by building an Episcopal church which was completed in the same year as the meeting house—1771.

The meeting house interior is now being restored to its original condition as a memorial to Israel Putnam, the man who was largely responsible for its construction—a man of great strength of mind and body, a hero of the Revolution. Possessed of indomitable courage, he once crawled into a wolf's cave on his hands and knees and killed the animal. The monument over his grave bears a replica of the head of a wolf and carved into the side are these words:

Passenger, if thou art a soldier, drop a tear over the dust of a Hero, who ever attentive to the lives of his men dared to lead where any dared to follow.

Old Trinity Church

EPISCOPAL

Brooklyn, Connecticut

Because of the animosity of two strong men toward each other, Brooklyn is blessed with two Colonial masterpieces, both built in 1771.

This charming edifice retains a feature common to the very early colonial days, the hip roof. It is located away from the village on a side road. The charm of the building, in which worship is now held only occasionally, is enhanced by the placidity of the old burying ground which surrounds it and the trees which shield it from the elements. The lovely entryway beckons invitingly from between trees and stones.

Among the headstones is a gently ironic reminder of the controversy which inspired the building of this church by Colonel Malbourne. One large marker bears the name Putnam. It was Israel Putnam who was Malbourne's chief adversary in that decade-long controversy.

It was not only the Congregationalist turned Unitarian who was filled with independence. The Episcopalian matched him ideal for ideal, faith for faith, building for building. Perhaps he is even one up, since there now is a new Episcopal church standing across from the old meeting house on the green.

The First Church of Christ

CONGREGATIONAL

Sharon, Connecticut

How amiable is Thy dwelling place, O Lord
    of Hosts!
Blessed are they that dwell in Thy house;
They will be always praising Thee.
               —Psalm 84

Facing the village green of Sharon, the First Church of Christ stands as a distinguished example of that flowering of New England architecture which took place in the early nineteenth century. The soft pink of the brick walls blends beautifully with the colors of the four seasons.

The congregation of the church was organized or "gathered" in 1739, but its first meeting house was not erected until 1742. With the growth of the congregation and the natural decay of the original building, a town meeting of October 16, 1766, voted to erect a new edifice. It was in this building that the Rev. Cotton Mather Smith served the congregation for fifty-two years. Here he preached a sermon of encouragement on the text "Watchman, what of the night? The watchman saith, The morning cometh!" Before the service was concluded, a runner dashed into the meeting house with the news of Burgoyne's surrender at Saratoga.

The interior of the present church has been restored to its original form and painted in the palest of grays, the whole effect creating an atmosphere of chaste simplicity and reverence. A unique feature is the curvature of the pews. In contrast to the more conventional straight pews, this seating gives a sense of intimacy and fellowship among the worshipers, and between pew and pulpit.

The true significance of a church building lies not in its history or its architectural merit, but in the living spirit that inhabits it. The congregation of the First Church of Christ believe this church to be vitally alive and its future to be as significant as its past.

The Congregational Church

Salisbury, Connecticut

The town of Salisbury has a distinctive character of independence which has roots in the beginnings of its Congregational church.

The ordination of the first minister, Jonathan Lee, was accomplished in 1744 outside the New Haven Consociation, which would normally have been its sanctioning body. But the Consociation represented the "Old Lights" Saybrook Platform, and Lee, licensed to preach by the "New Lights" New London Association, had determined to be ordained by a council according to the Cambridge Platform of the "New Lights." The town stood solidly behind Lee.

The three ministers who ordained Lee were members of the New Haven Consociation, which punished them for their action by withdrawing from them the privilege of fellowship. Two of these ministers subsequently confessed error and were restored to membership. The charge against the third ordainer, an extremely popular man, must have been dropped, as he was restored to good standing without having made any confession of error.

The church of Salisbury and its "Saints," as the organizers of churches were called, being outside the Consociation, were, like their minister, outside its power to punish by excommunication.

The first meeting house was the log house built by the town as the residence for the minister, who built more sophisticated quarters as soon as he could.

The second meeting house, completed in 1752, still stands as the central area of the Salisbury Town Hall, a building in which town meetings have been held since that early date.

The present church, completed in 1800, stands directly across the road from the parent building, which at night beams a light to its steeple.

First Congregational Church

Litchfield, Connecticut

All aspects of this magnificent restoration are beautiful. It is one of the most photographed buildings in the country. The exterior is perfectly proportioned, the interior is a harmony of gracious simplicity. The pulpit and Communion table are the acme of the cabinet-maker's art.

Yet, all of this beauty was abandoned in 1873 in favor of a wooden, pseudo-Gothic Victorian structure; abandoned to serve the community as armory, dance hall, theater, basketball court and movie house. While these uses seem hardly fitting for an architectural gem, we can be grateful that such continuous use of the building resulted in its preservation until the day in 1929 when restoration was begun.

One of the highlights of the restoration was the duplication of the original pulpit. Two older members of the congregation drew pictures of the pulpit as they remembered it. Their impressions proved to be almost exactly identical.

From the base of a table found nearby came three of the pulpit volutes and segments of the stair rails, and the base of the original Communion table top provided parts of the pillars. The fourth volute was found in a pile of rubbish. These segments, together with the drawings, made possible the reproduction of the original pulpit.

One of the old pew doors was found in the basement and from it the size and type of the pews were determined and the present doors reproduced.

Four of the pillars which support the gallery are exact reproductions, undistinguishable from the originals.

After a long and frustrating search for the original weather vane, it was found just across the common in the Historical Society Museum, which also provided the two pulpit lamps.

All difficulties and frustrations were overcome by the love and devotion of those responsible for bringing back a late Colonial masterpiece.

Church of Christ

CONGREGATIONAL

Norfolk, Connecticut

Norfolk stands on the coldest hills of Connecticut, where the snow and ice lie deep on greenwood and slope. Here, in 1787, the Thanksgiving Day sermon was interrupted by a youth who announced that a hunt was on for a family of wolves which had been depredating the area. From his pulpit, the minister immediately seconded the appeal for assistance, whereupon "a great part of the male members rose from their seats and flew to the scene of the action." The hunt was concluded with the extermination of the wolves. No mention is made in the church history as to the conclusion of the sermon.

A difficult case of offense against the church, tried here by church council, was that of a member who "professed the doctrine of poligamy, though he did not practice it." (Since five people were involved in the case, the reader is left to conjecture as to the actual practice of the "doctrine.")

The first minister, Ammi Robbins, in addition to carrying out his church work, prepared more than 100 scholars for entrance to college. His effectiveness as a teacher was symbolized by the presentation to him of a gold watch by one of his grateful students. The watch, with its gold key, has been passed from minister to succeeding minister with a photostatic copy of the presentation letter. This treasured tradition of the Norfolk church is to be continued without limit of time.

The South Canaan Congregational Church

MEMBER OF THE CHURCH ASSOCIATION

South Canaan, Connecticut

Erected in 1804, this church is now used only in the summer months because of its lack of heat, water, electricity and congregation. The summer, however, brings loyal worshipers from as far away as Hartford.

South Canaan is now a member of the Church Association that includes the Falls Village Congregational and the Falls Village Methodist churches, which are also used seasonally to provide year-round worship for the Protestant community.

Much early church construction was paid for by the sale of pews. South Canaan used another popular device designed to raise the necessary money. They held a lottery. But it is doubtful that the church derived any financial benefit from this venture. Lotteries, in those days, were subject to chicanery and embezzlement. It appears that this lottery did not avoid the pitfall of avarice. It is known that there was no squaring of accounts for twenty-six years, long after the church construction had been otherwise paid for.

In 1938, when Route 7 was rebuilt, it was discovered that the center of the state road right of way passed directly through the center of the church from front door to pulpit. The state did not exercise its right of fee, and relocated the road a comfortable distance from the church building.

Catholic Church of St. Mary

ROMAN CATHOLIC

Lakeville, Connecticut

The town of Salisbury, of which Lakeville is a part, was the center of iron mining and converting activities of the Colonies and the United States until after the Civil War. Many of the iron workers of the area were Roman Catholics who, for a long time, had no church of their own.

The first Mass celebrated in Lakeville was said on July 4, 1849, under a tree near the old Davis iron mine.

Reverend Christopher Moore, the first resident pastor in the area, assumed his charge in 1850. Having no church in which to gather his flock of iron workers, Father Moore said Mass in private homes and, for a short time, at the Amesville schoolhouse. It was said that the residue of Protestant resentment against anything Papist was responsible for the locking of the schoolhouse against such use; but it is equally likely that another cause was the zealous guarding of the traditional separation of church and state which had become cherished in this part of the country. Indeed, the Methodists were also locked out after a short use of the same building, the reason given in their case being that "the loud singing was a disturbance."

Through continued service of Mass in private homes and in the open air, the church was kept alive, and by 1875 St. Mary's was built on land which Congregationalists had made available to the Catholic parish.

The chief benefactors of the young church were Jonathan Scoville (a wealthy Protestant) and the Hon. William Barnum (organizer of the Lime Rock Episcopal church), "who was ever a generous and consistent friend."

Trinity Church

EPISCOPAL

Lime Rock, Connecticut

As a part of Salisbury, Lime Rock was also engaged in the iron industry. The Barnum and Richardson foundry, which manufactured railroad car wheels, was located here on Salmon Fell Kill. William Barnum, an important Connecticut political figure, was inspired by his wife to assist in the organizing of Trinity Church in 1873. Mrs. Barnum, along with others, felt that the then arduous trip to Salisbury village each Sunday was a deterrent to the devotion of many Lime Rock residents.

The church was consecrated on November 5, 1874. It was lighted by gas produced in a pit on the church grounds. At an evening service the lights suddenly went out and the minister, holding a lighted lantern, opened the pit to investigate the cause of the failure. The resultant explosion almost killed him. On his recovery, his attending physician told his patient that he ought to have known that fire would burn a minister in this world if it wouldn't in the next.

A few years ago, the idyllic quiet of Lime Rock was shattered in several ways by the construction, directly across the road from the church, of Lime Rock Park, a sports-car race track. Sunday morning church services were disrupted by the lack of parking space for the churchgoers and by the roar of the speeding cars. The ensuing controversy between religious and recreational interests was settled by a court injunction, which proscribed Sunday activities at the track. The faithful of Trinity Church were once again enabled to worship in their accustomed peace and quiet.

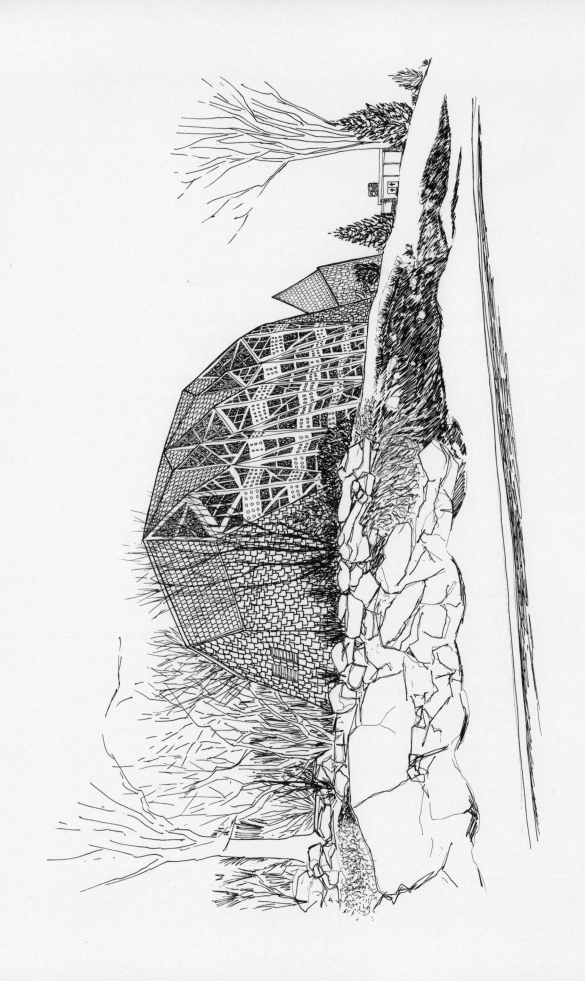

The First Presbyterian Church

Stamford, Connecticut

This congregation, which dedicated its first church in 1854, completed its architecturally unique edifice in 1958. It is famous through the world as the "Fish Church," because it is built in the shape of a fish, whose backbone stands the equivalent of six stories from the ground.

It is appropriate, for many reasons, that a Christian church should take this form. Until 500 A.D., when the cross became accepted as the symbol of Christianity, it was the fish which served that purpose. *Ichthus* is the Greek word for fish, and the first letters of the words "Jesus Christ, God's Son, Saviour" form this word in the Greek language.

The magnificent windows, formed of inch-thick stained glass, carved to give texture to the transmitted light, are a remarkable combination of nonrepresentational and representational art.

The lighting units are designed and hung as unobtrusive mobiles which quietly grace the air space of the nave.

The electronic organ is the largest in the world. With its more than one hundred stops and thousands of individual electronic circuits it produces the majestic tones of the diapason and the sound effects of orchestral instruments. Only six organs in the world can produce the "state trumpet" sound, which requires fifty times as much air pressure as any other sound. The music of the organ is projected from both ends of the interior.

The complex of buildings is designed to serve the congregation from basinette to adulthood. All educational, recreational and worship needs of a religious community are provided for here.

The Cathedral of St. Joseph

ROMAN CATHOLIC

Hartford, Connecticut

The last day of the year 1956 dawned cold and gray. In Hartford, Mass was celebrated for the last time in the old Cathedral of St. Joseph. By midafternoon the massive edifice was a smoking ruin. The mother church of the Archdiocese of Hartford, erected by other generations of Connecticut Catholics as a tribute of love and loyalty to their Creator, was no more. Shock and sorrow numbed the hearts and minds of priests and people.

Thus, with the words of Archbishop Henry J. O'Brien, begins the dedication book of the new Cathedral of St. Joseph, opened with the Pontifical Mass celebrated May 23, 1962, at 10:30 A.M.

It is a building with one foot in the architectural and traditional past and the other in the present. There is no decoration, as this term is commonly used. Everything which might be styled decoration is, in fact, integral to the building. The iconographic theme, for example, is carried in the doors, the windows, the reredos, the altarpieces and the mosaics. The stations of the cross are cut directly into the piers which form the side aisles without breaking the open space of the nave or obstructing the view of altar and sanctuary.

Across the avenue is the Home Office Building of the Aetna Affiliated Companies, the largest Colonial-type structure in the world. From 1957 through 1959, the parish of St. Joseph was given the use of the Aetna auditorium for three Masses each Sunday.

St. Mark's Parish

EPISCOPAL

New Canaan, Connecticut

One of the important aspects of contemporary religious architecture is the inspiration and outlet it provides for designers, sculptors, painters and weavers. Religion has long been a key source of inspiration for great art, but architecture has not always provided either additional inspiration or a home for the products of artistic creativity. We are fortunate to live in an area of time in which architecture does provide both home and stimulus for art which enriches our worship and our culture.

St. Mark's is one of the many contemporary church buildings which house an abundance of fine art. The light inside is enriched by the windows through which it passes. The kneeling cushions around the free-standing altar are glorified by the weaver's art. The lattice reredos behind the altar is resplendent with hundreds of metal sculptures hung in a design both beautiful and symbolic.

The total visual and spiritual effect of St. Mark's is a tribute to man's ability to serve tradition without being enslaved by it.

St. Joseph's Church

ROMAN CATHOLIC

Canaan, Connecticut

The cause of the Roman Church in northwest Connecticut was well served by the redoubtable Father Peter Kelly, who succeeded Father Christopher Moore in 1851. Father Kelly was a charming, cane-wielding, militant realist who was successful in bringing about a greater acceptance of the presence of Catholic worship in the area—so successful that the superintendent of the Amesville iron works, ignorant of the priest's vows of celibacy, offered Father Kelly his daughter's hand in marriage. The priest simply referred the man to the Bishop, whose visit was imminent, to "get his approval of the marriage." The next time Father Kelly saw the indignant superintendent he was to hear: "Your boss is a stubborn and unreasonable man; also a dunce. He could not understand, nor would he listen to my explanation; he dismissed me without hearing all that I was prepared to propose." The Bishop, in relating the story, often alluded to the priest as "that rascal Kelly."

By 1854 Father Kelly, who in deference to the Protestant community never wore a Roman collar, had succeeded in building a church and paying for it— his mother in Ireland helping him to free it of all encumbrance. It was this church of which St. Joseph's was a mission till it became a mission of St. Mary's in Lakeville.

In 1920 St. Joseph's was made a parish church, and in 1940 the present church was dedicated. It is a modern interpretation of early Irish architecture, of a simplicity chosen to harmonize with its New England setting. The interior is equally simple and charming in its soft light, transmitted by the windows of varying shades of blue antique glass, in which are set panels of stained-glass allegories, six of which serve in this book as section separators.

Holy Trinity Church

RUSSIAN ORTHODOX

New Britain, Connecticut

The beginnings of Holy Trinity parish go back to the turn of the twentieth century when a small group of Russians from Austro-Hungary formed the SS. Cyril and Methodius Brotherhood. The original organizational efforts attempted to bring together Uniate and Galician groups. These efforts were unsuccessful. There were, however, some White Russians living among the Poles of the city who consented to join the Brotherhood, which was further augmented in numbers by Poles who followed the Russian Orthodox faith.

By 1914 the present building, a fine example of Russian Orthodox ecclesiastical architecture with its onion-shaped cupolas, was built and given the name Holy Trinity. The year 1961 brought the installation of imported stained-glass windows unique in this country; they are done in the fifteenth-century Rublovian (Russian Byzantine) style.

Some of the older members of the congregation still carry on correspondence with relatives in Russia or Poland. They receive interesting bits of information which are sometimes viewed with a measure of skepticism. The dried mushrooms, which also come from Eastern Europe in the mail, are a gourmet's delight. They are welcomed without skepticism.

The people of Holy Trinity are among those who keep alive the traditions of the Russia that existed before the Bolshevik Revolution. These are Russians who, when they chose another form of government in preference to Czarist tyranny, chose democracy and freedom of speech and worship.

St. Thomas Assyrian Church

HOLY APOSTOLIC AND CATHOLIC CHURCH OF THE EAST

New Britain, Connecticut

The Assyrians who established this congregation in 1919 came from the Azerbaijan area of northwest Iran. The first of these immigrants arrived around 1910, intending to make their fortunes in the Golden Land and take these gains back to benefit the lot of the Assyrians in the homeland. The outbreak of World War One and the subsequent persecution of Assyrians discouraged such return and, in fact, occasioned further emigration to the New World.

The Assyrians were of the ancient Judaic tribes who became known as Mesopotamian Jews. Unlike the Jews of Palestine, the Assyrians believed in the Divinity of Christ's person and Messianic mission. They offered Christ refuge among them. They were the first total ethnic group to accept the Gospel of Jesus Christ as their religion, and they founded the first organized Christian Church, the Church of the East. Such organization was possible because the Zoroastrian Persians offered no resistance to the new faith, which was practiced openly without the persecutions common in other areas.

It is sometimes thought that Nestorius was the founder of the Church of the East, but it had already been in existence for hundreds of years when Nestorius was charged with heresy by the Byzantine church. He was welcomed by the Assyrians, who believed that his positions were theologically correct and proper.

The language of the church, its people and its scriptures is the Aramaic spoken by Christ and the Apostles. The form and tenets of the faith have remained unchanged from the original. It is felt by many that these *untranslated* words are the pure, undiluted teachings of Jesus Christ as he spoke them.

St. Thomas More House

THE ROMAN CATHOLIC CHAPEL AND CENTER IN YALE UNIVERSITY

New Haven, Connecticut

St. Thomas More House provides the first Roman Catholic Chapel for the Yale students of that faith. Mass is celebrated every day of the year, but More House is more than church and chapel—it is also a center for meetings, seminars and social activities.

St. Thomas More, the patron saint of lawyers, was a man of tremendous scope in the England of the fifteenth and sixteenth centuries. Educated at Oxford, he rose to eminence as a lawyer, was under-sheriff of London, and was elected a burgess of the Parliament under Henry VII, where he was often successful in resisting claims of the Crown. In 1514 and 1515 he was sent on embassies to The Netherlands. After his return he became a privy councillor. In 1523 he was chosen speaker of the House of Commons and he became Lord Chancellor in 1529, holding the great seal for two and a half years.

The fullness of his political and public activities did not prevent his achievements as a literary figure of great stature. His *Utopia,* a romantic dream of the perfect society, is a classic statement of humanism.

Thomas More constantly refused to lend his authority to Henry VIII's project of divorce and remarriage. In 1534 he refused to swear allegiance to the Act of Succession for securing the throne to the offspring of Anne Boleyn and was committed to the Tower of London. In July 1535, having refused to acknowledge Henry VIII as supreme head of the Church over the Pope, he was charged with treason, condemned and executed. So ended a life of singular faithfulness to principles of religion, law and ethics.

The Unitarian Church in Westport

Westport, Connecticut

The First Unitarian Society of Fairfield County began in 1949 with a starting group of twelve. Eleven years later the Society dedicated this soaring structure on a rocky, wooded knoll in the outskirts of Westport and took its present name.

The congregation thinks of it as the "new Ship Church" as contrasted with the "old Ship Church" of Hingham, Massachusetts. Coincidentally, the minister here was raised in the Hingham area.

This is a "live" congregation whose activities are many and constantly manifest in the spacious facilities. It is not just a Sunday building or Sunday group. The nursery school lilts with the sounds of children at their learning play. The walls glow with the exhibition paintings hung on them. The offices ring with correspondence being typed and the air is warmed by the interracial harmony which radiates from this place of reverence for God and man.

Light sidles in from glass walls and pours down from the transparent strip which joins the two roof sections, as though to illumine the heart and mind with nature's beauty.

The sweeping lines speak of an upward striving toward a promise of the unity which is the faith of the people who built this structure.

Church of the Sacred Heart

ROMAN CATHOLIC

Hartford, Connecticut

Many churches have served more than one congregation, more than one faith, or more than one ethnic group. Sacred Heart exemplifies the enduring universality of religion for it has, within one faith, served three distinct groups.

The church was brought into being to fill the religious needs of German Catholics who emigrated to America and settled in Hartford. The congregation numbered about 150 families, many of whose older descendants remain attached by the ties which bind worshipers to a particular church. Some of these people were baptized and confirmed here, took their first Communion here, were married here, and celebrated Requiem Masses for parents here. Such continuity is not easily broken.

The change of the neighborhood's ethnic character from German-American to Italian-American was reflected in Sacred Heart's congregation. Italian or German, educated or unlettered, skilled or unskilled, the immigrants were welcomed by a land which needed their services—a land with time to be patient while new citizens learned its language, a land of unlimited opportunity even for the limited.

All of this has changed. The patience is gone, the tempo is quickened, opportunities for the limited have almost vanished. Technology has no appetite for the unskilled or unschooled. There is very little employment for Hartford's newest residents, the Spanish-speaking Puerto Rican Americans who now make up the greater part of Sacred Heart parish. In a prosperous city, the neighborhood has become an enclave of economic distress where lack of opportunity breeds indolence, despair and trouble; and where children are destined, it seems, for lives out of step with technocracy's rapid pace. The church works hard to help its people, but, like them, it is limited. It cannot provide the jobs which would give rebirth to the hopes which brought these Puerto Ricans to Hartford.

First Unitarian Congregational Society of Hartford

Hartford, Connecticut

Dedicated in the first snow of the winter, on December 6, 1964, this meeting house was designed as a "living" building to symbolize, as a structure, the individuality and variety to which the Unitarian principle of freedom leads.

The architect said: "Unitarians believe there are many approaches to the truth that unites them. I tried in this church for a symbolic and lyrical interpretation of the Unitarian Church."

The meeting house rises naturally from its environment. The natural state of the structural materials displays their honest qualities. The twelve irregularly spaced radial walls of concrete soar to different heights, rising like a magnificent updraft of spirituality.

The multiple entries testify to the inclusiveness of the human brotherhood aimed at in the Unitarian faith.

The centrality of the sanctuary expresses the unity of the congregation and the inward quietness of worship.

These lines appear in a book of meditations on a table in the church narthex:

> I am an individual and, thus, unique.
> I can choose if I will.
> I can reflect upon my yesterdays and use them now
> To make of my tomorrows something more.

United Church of Christ

CONGREGATIONAL

West Norwalk, Connecticut

Though this church gives the visual impression of a multi-faceted Trinity, such an effect was not the conscious intent of the architect, Victor Christ-Janer. He says: "One tragedy of our times is that esthetics can be and are conditioned by the media of mass communications and the facility of travel, which combine to overexpose us to repetitive statements which create unrelated fashions; our concern must be a search for more profoundly related concepts which will express the continuity of man's struggles and tensions and his various reactions to them."

The personal discipline to which the architect has subjected himself is reflected in the fragmentation of both the interior and exterior of this building. Yet, this fragmentation has been so designed that it results in a remarkable unity which changes and changes with the viewing of each aspect. Since there is no single façade, these aspects are almost limitless.

There is a thorny sharpness here as a reminder that life is not all sweetness and simple harmony. The architectural dissonance is visually reminiscent of the music of Aaron Copland and Igor Stravinsky.

Christ-Janer has searched for a solution which is not spatially "resolved" because the Protestant faith itself is unresolved in that it provides no ultimate solution in man's religious search. The three small drawings show the principle stages of Christ-Janer's thinking toward the Christian Protestant church structure. The first represents the completely resolved form of the Catholic or Apostolic enclosure; the second represents the basic duality and tension which is life itself—good and evil, peace and war, noise and quiet, black and white. The third represents the fragmentation which is spatially unresolved and leaves open the way to new growth and form.

The church looks like a great land-bound iceberg, the greater part of which is unseen, deep below the surface of a sea of soil and rock.

RHODE ISLAND

Hope

The First Baptist Meeting House

Providence, Rhode Island

For the Publick Worship of Almighty God; and also for holding Commencement In.

This church is the oldest of any denomination in Rhode Island and the oldest Baptist church in America. It was founded in 1638 by Roger Williams and his companions, who had broken away from the established order in the Massachusetts Colony. Here, on land they purchased from the Indians, they founded a colony in which they themselves might enjoy and also offer "to all men of distressed conscience the priceless boon of soul-liberty." To this day the church has no formal creed or covenant.

Roger Williams, believing that Christendom had been corrupted and the rites of the church had become invalid, withdrew from the church after only a few months.

The present building was erected in 1775 and is eighty feet square, with entry doors on the four sides. The large size was required to accommodate the general community meetings and the Brown University Commencements held here.

The 185-foot steeple is modeled from designs by James Gibbs, a pupil of Christopher Wren. It was built in telescopic sections on the ground by ship's carpenters who were idled by the shipping blockade imposed by the British.

This church represents the first important break from the colonial church-state entente. Roger Williams was banished from Massachusetts Colony because he believed in true religious freedom for all men—"The civil magistrate's power extends only to the bodies and goods and outward state of men. No person should be compelled to pray or pay, otherwise than as his soul believeth and consenteth."

Quaker Meeting House

Newport, Rhode Island

Of the seventeenth-century New England buildings, almost none remain, so it is sadly ironic that the Quakers, so important to the early development of Newport, are no longer here in sufficient numbers to maintain a meeting house. The house they built in 1699 still stands. It is used as the Community Center for underprivileged children of Newport. It is in a sad state of disrepair, which seems to demonstrate a lack of proper civic respect for either the historical importance of the building or the work which it now houses.

In 1706, George Keith wrote:

The Quaker had built a new meeting house at Newport, large enough to hold Five Hundred Persons or more, with fair and large Galleries, and Forms or Benches below. But one thing singular I observed, that on the *top of the turret* of their meeting house, they have a *perfect iron cross, two large Iron Bars crossing one the other at right Angles,* a more perfect Cross I never saw on any Church.

The iron cross which Keith described so "perfidiously accepted" by the Quakers, is actually formed by the braces of the turret and was not intended as a religious symbol.

The upper part of the ell at the north of the building is noteworthy because of its curved and cased ceiling timbers, which caused it to be known as "the Old Ship Room," an appropriate structuring in a seafaring community.

The Quaker Meeting House and the stone Newport Tower are the only surviving nondomestic buildings of seventeenth-century Newport.

The Newport Tower

Newport, Rhode Island

The Newport Tower has been the subject of extensive controversy, archaeological and historical investigation, and resultant literature.

It is a substantially cylindrical tower about twenty-three feet in diameter and about twenty-six feet in overall height. The upper part is a solid wall with windows and port openings. Precise dimensions are more readily obtained through measurement in old Norse feet than through the use of English feet.

The design of the stone Tower proves adequate for a particular type of church structure. The windows, port openings and fireplace form a sophisticated signaling and ship guidance system characteristic of the fourteenth-century Norsemen.

There are three basic schools of thought about the origin of the Tower. One of these is that it was built by Governor Benedict Arnold; another, supported by the "prototype" theory, contends that it was erected at an unknown early date by a Viking group; the third believes that Portuguese explorers, possibly Cortereal, were the builders. The most romantic of these theories is that Norsemen, possibly Eric, Bishop of Gardar in Greenland, built the Tower in the twelfth century as a combination church, lighthouse and navigation guide.

All of this is, at this time, conjecture; some professional, some amateur, some emotional, some romantic. No archaeological or historical evidence has thus far been uncovered to support or deny the validity of any of the contentions or theories which have been advanced about the Newport Tower. So the possibility still exists that this might have been America's oldest place of Christian worship.

Touro Synagogue of Congregation Jeshuat Israel

JUDAIC ORTHODOX

A National Historic Site

Newport, Rhode Island

Jews of Spain and Portugal, the Sephardim, under the scourge of the Inquisition, along with the Marranos, who had cloaked themselves with ostensible conversion to Christianity, heard in Europe of the freedom of religion in the Rhode Island Colony, and as early as 1658, they came to Newport, where they formed a congregation according to Hebrew tradition. They were joined by Ashkenazim from Eastern and Central Europe. The two groups swallowed their traditional differences to form one religious community which began its synagogue construction in 1759. It is the oldest synagogue in North America, its only predecessor, in New York, having been demolished.

In 1790 this congregation received from George Washington a letter which is a classic declaration of religious liberty:

... The citizens of the USA have a right to applaud themselves for having given to mankind examples of an enlarged and liberal policy: a policy worthy of imitation. All possess alike liberty of conscience and immunities of citizenship. It is now no more that toleration is spoken of, as if it was by the indulgence of one class of people, that another enjoyed the exercise of their inherited natural rights. For happily the Government of the United States, which gives to bigotry no sanction, to persecution no assistance, requires only that they who live under its protection should demean themselves as good citizens, in giving it on all occasions their effectual support.

... May the children of the Stock of Abraham, who dwell in this land, continue to merit and enjoy the good will of the other inhabitants; while every one shall sit in safety under his own vine and fig tree, and there shall be none to make him afraid.

These words preceded the Bill of Rights by more than a year.

Trinity Church

EPISCOPAL

Newport, Rhode Island

Newport provides more than ample evidence of the rich rewards of Rhode Island's traditional freedom of religion. One of the most beautiful of these examples is Trinity Church, built in 1726, twenty-eight years after the congregation was organized.

Richard Munday, Newport's Master Carpenter, incorporated into the structure the most important features of Christopher Wren's famous London churches. It is possible that Wren drew the original plans from which Munday worked.

Trinity has been called "a supreme and matchless reminder of colonial America." No major wooden structure of early colonial days has been so well preserved. Trinity is the fourth Church of England parish to have been established north of the Mason-Dixon line. It was organized largely by Huguenots who had fled the persecutions to which they had been subjected in France. These men, reacting unfavorably to the excesses of Puritanism which culminated in the Salem witchcraft panic of 1692, joined with a handful of Colonists loyal to the Church of England.

Many treasures contribute to Trinity's fame as an unsurpassed colonial heritage, among them the baptismal font, hammered from a single sheet of silver. It is possibly America's finest piece of silverware.

The bell in the Tower Room is thought to have been the first church bell sounded in New England.

Eighty books received from England in 1701 formed the first parish library of Rhode Island.

The organ was installed in 1733, the second such instrument in all America.

The black and gold altarpiece has been in place since 1733, although the British royal coat of arms which surmounted it was destroyed after the British evacuated Newport.

Seventh Day Baptist Meeting House

SABBATARIAN

Newport, Rhode Island

Attached to the north wall of this meeting house, to the right of the pulpit, is a bronze tablet on which is inscribed:

TO THE MEMORY OF

Wm. Hiscox, Stephen Mumford, Samuel Hubbard, Roger Baster, Sister Hubbard, Sister Mumford, Sister Rachel Langworthy, &C., who for greater freedom in the exercise of religious faith in the observance of God's Holy Sabbath the Seventh day of the week, reluctantly severed their connection with the parent Church of Newport; and "Entered into a Church covt. the 23rd day of Dec. 1671" (old style: January 3, 1672 New style). Thereby establishing the Seventh Day Baptist Church of that faith in the world. It was sometimes called the Third Baptist Church of Newport and was the Seventh Baptist Church to be organized in America.

This House of worship was erected in 1729 under the direction of Jonathan Weeden and Henry Collins.

The observance of the seventh day as the Sabbath, in Newport, dates back to 1664, when Stephen Mumford came from London and brought with him the opinion that the whole of the Ten Commandments, as they were delivered from Mount Sinai, were moral and immutable. Several members of the First Church in Newport embraced this sentiment, but nevertheless stayed with that church till 1671.

Newport being a center of the slave-running, rum-shipping industry, it is noteworthy that Parson Thurston, the pastor of this church for forty-two years and a cooper, absolutely refused "to use his craft for the manufacture of any description of cask used in the shipment of New England rum to the coast."

From 1864 to 1869 the meeting house was occupied by the Shiloh Baptist Church, a Negro congregation which subsequently purchased the former parish school building from the Trinity Corporation.

The Sabbatarian history of the building is kept alive by an annual service.

Mt. Zion African Methodist Episcopal Church

Newport, Rhode Island

African Methodism exists as a protest against the segregation that once prevailed in many Christian churches.

In 1787 the Negroes of Philadelphia who belonged to that city's Methodist Society were treated as nuisances in the house of worship, to the extent that they were pulled from their knees while in the act of prayer and ordered to the back seats. Because of these and other acts of un-Christian conduct, they considered it their duty to build a house of their own.

They met with great resistance from the elders of the Methodist Church, who threatened them with expulsion from the Society. Instead of meekly complying with the demands of the Society, they sent in their resignations.

By 1793 their number had increased sufficiently to proceed with the building of their church on land owned by a former slave. Threats did not stop the project, and when the building was finally complete the Methodist Bishop accepted an invitation to open the house for divine worship. Immediately after the opening there followed further efforts to discourage and upset the congregation until the final break was made and the name African Methodist Episcopal Church was adopted.

From its small beginning this Church has spread through this country to the Indies, South America and Africa.

Mt. Zion was organized in 1845 with sixteen members. By 1853 it had purchased its own property. The present church, formerly the Touro Academy of Music, located adjacent to the very old Jewish Burying Ground, was bought in 1875. It is the oldest Negro congregation in Newport.

Temple Beth El

JUDAIC REFORMED

Providence, Rhode Island

Temple Beth El is one of the oldest Hebrew congregations in the country. It is a large temple, with over one thousand families as members. The imposing structure has many noteworthy features, such as the four entrance terrace mosaics, the exterior Menorah sculpture, the sanctuary curtains, the metal-sculptured pillar of cloud and pillar of fire which flank the ark, and the Biblical garden.

The central feature of the garden is the stone tablets from the congregation's first temple. They are fronted by a mulberry tree, considered the wisest of trees because it does not put forth its buds until all threat of frost is past. Then they all seem to pop simultaneously.

Pyracantha (firethorn) is espaliered in the form of the seven-branched candelabrum, the Menorah. It has been said that "Moses saw this plant in the wilderness and had the candlesticks made for his Tabernacle."

The ground cover of myrtle is a symbol of the myrtle which grows in the Holy Land, named "Hadas." Queen Esther was named for it because of her sweetness and purity: she was called "Hadassah."

Saffron crocuses, as a symbol of the Jewish ability to rise and flourish after adversity, love to be trodden on and grow fairer when the root is crushed into the ground.

Juniper and sycamore were the woods most used by the ancient Jews until Solomon selected the cedars of Lebanon.

Rue and wormwood, bitter but good, suggest the bitterness, disappointment and remorse so familiar in Jewish history.

Sage, symbolizing profound wisdom and philosophy, grows under the weeping willow tree, likened to godlike people who acquire spiritual knowledge quickly.

The winged Euonymous Alatus represents the burning bush. The nearby bittersweet vines are being trained in the shape of angel's wings.

The garden was created to make of the Bible a living thing to be brought out beyond the doors of Synagogue and Church—not pedantry, but Fruition! The minds of men turned *only* Godward do not hear the voices of serpents and thus cannot be subverted.

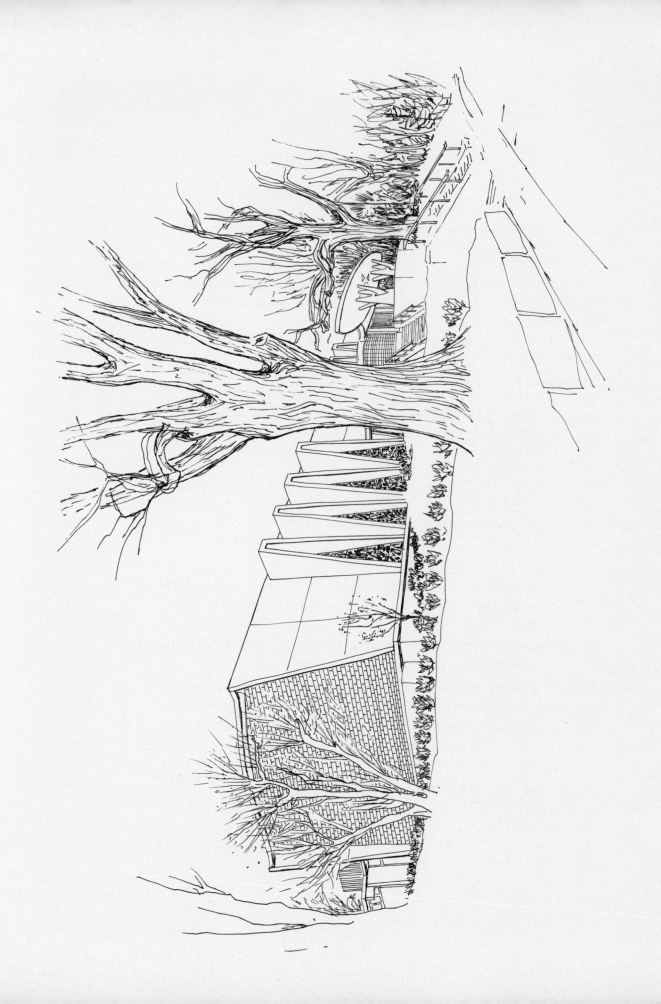

Congregation B'nai Israel

JUDAIC CONSERVATIVE SYNAGOGUE AND COMMUNITY CENTER

Woonsocket, Rhode Island

And I will look upon it, that I may remember the everlasting covenant between God and every living creature.

B'nai Israel is new and dazzling to the eye, but it is a century old in the dreams of its congregation. It is the first house of worship to be built by the Jews of Woonsocket. For fifty-eight years of that century, a former Presbyterian church housed the congregation. As they worshiped through the decades in facilities purchased from their Christian neighbors, they cherished the hope that one day they should be the hosts to rather than the guests of other great faiths. Today, the synagogue is open to all who wish to visit these beautiful facilities for worship or hospitality.

What the fathers set out to do so long ago the sons and daughters have accomplished, in the building of an edifice calculated to strengthen spiritual life and to bring cultural enrichment to the entire community—a tribute to both the sacred traditions of Hebraic heritage and the cherished traditions of brotherhood of the Republic.

That this small congregation of about two hundred families was able to achieve such a magnificent fulfillment of Judaic worship is remarkable in itself. The totality of its beauty reflects an unusual harmony of sensitivity, culture and good taste. The Star of David in the entry canopy may shine proudly on this work, built to honor the Woonsocket Jewish service men and women—a testimony of love of country coupled with love of God.

NEW HAMPSHIRE

Live free or die

Park Hill Meeting House

UNITED

Westmoreland, New Hampshire

This lovely old building was erected in 1764 as a Congregational church and meeting house. It is not, as are so many colonial churches, a restoration. The floors of two-foot-wide pine planking are anything but flat. There are few of the later-day refinements of furnishings.

The four great columns were hand-turned on a crude lathe from trees cut in the woods to the north of the church. Approximately thirty feet tall and eighteen to twenty inches in diameter at the bases, there is less than a quarter of an inch difference in their sizes.

So unique is the construction and framing of the steeple that in 1953 the Weyerhauser Company of Everett, Washington, sent two of its engineers to make a chart of its framework and timbers for the American White Pine Association. The bell housed in the steeple is one of the original Paul Revere bells.

The 1791 Communion set of Park Hill consists of fifteen beautiful pieces of fine pewter created by such renowned English and American pewterers as Robert Bush and Nathaniel Austin. The marks on the six cups are very rare and are highly prized. Few churches have the distinction of owning a set so complete and of such estimable workmanship.

The present minister is Congregational, but the bylaws of this United church provide for rotation of denominational representation by successive ministers.

Bedford Presbyterian Church

Bedford, New Hampshire

The Presbyterian Church of Bedford was organized in 1749, a year before the Town, by a group of Scotch-Irish settlers who had moved up from Londonderry. Until they built their own church these sturdy people walked, children in arms, a distance of twelve miles and canoed across the river to their regular worship. It is said of them that they "never gave up a pint of rum or a p'int of scripture." Officialdom of colonial days was not able to deprive them of their own house of worship, which was until a year ago the only church in Bedford. In 1784 a special clause in the legislature relieved Bedford townsfolk from public assessment toward the support of the Congregational Church.

In the seventeen-hundreds the Rev. Mr. Houston and his neighbor Riddle had a serious and vituperative quarrel about fence lines. The next day Mr. Riddle was questioned about his presence in church after such an altercation with the minister. His answer was: "My quarrel was with the minister, not his gospel."

An early minister who was outspoken in his Tory sympathies was got rid of by the congregation by giving him a year's vacation—without pay.

The present church, built in 1832 at a cost of less than $3,000, is a beautiful example of late Colonial architecture in a remarkable state of preservation.

Shaker Meeting House

THE UNITED SOCIETY OF BELIEVERS IN CHRIST'S SECOND APPEARING

Shaker Village, Canterbury, New Hampshire

Situated at the head of a lane of majestic maples on a high hill outside the village of Canterbury is the old meeting house of the Shaker village which was established here in 1792.

This order of celibate Believers was established in America in Niskayuna, New York, in 1774. Societies were soon established throughout New England. One of the Believers, Moses Johnson, a fine craftsman in wood, became the Society's architect. It was he who designed and built the meeting houses, of which this is a fine example.

The meeting houses had two doors, one for men, the other for ladies, though part of the creed of the Believers is the equality of the sexes. Benches lined the walls, leaving the meeting room free for the marching and dancing which were an essential part of the early rituals of Believers' worship. The hands were extended, palms up, as a sign of receiving love from the powers above. The march step indicated their going on the way of God, the dances their joy in the Lord. The shaking movements which were part of the dance brought the appellation "The Shaking Quakers." Like the Quakers, the Shakers are pacifist. Like the Quakers, the Shakers have made their name a symbol of dignity with no trace of the derision with which it was originally applied.

Sister Margaret Frost has written of the order:

Down through the stream of time small so-called heretical groups kept alive what seemed to them a more real approach to the life taught by Christ Jesus than did the staticity of the institutional churches. In the prose of human existence they felt the poetry of heavenly living.

The Shaker bywords are: "Hands to work and hearts to God."

The Congregational Church

Amherst, New Hampshire

In what is one of the oldest and loveliest villages of New Hampshire, the unique steeple of the Congregational Church stands high over the village common.

In colonial and post-colonial days the cost of building and up-keep of the meeting house and the wages of the preacher were raised through property assessments and taxes levied by the town assessors. This lasted until a little after 1800, when Dr. John Mussey of Amherst refused to pay 75¢ assessed him for current parish charges and $2.23 for the preacher's salary. He was jailed and finally paid the tax, under protest. His subsequent lawsuit against the assessors to recover the money and costs was tried and decided in his favor by the Superior Court in Amherst in May of 1803. The suit cost the parish $250. Dr. Mussey was a Presbyterian who objected to supporting a Congregational church. His action began the real separation of church and state in New England.

In 1828 the total separation of the church from the town took place, and in 1832 the Congregational Church and Society was organized, buying the church property from the town, the terms of sale being: "1st the Town to reserve the Bell, Clocks and Belfry or Tower as the property of the Town; the purchaser to have the right to pass and repass through the west doors as now used—also to ring the Bell for funerals, public worship and other public occasions without expense to the Town."

In the usual instance, the Congregational Meeting House was considered the property of the church and was often given to the town when a new church structure was erected.

Free Baptist Church

Wilmot Flat, New Hampshire

The church background of Wilmot emphasizes the struggle for denominational recognition in the early years of our country. It was in 1804 that the New Hampshire legislature granted to Freewill Baptists the right to be considered a distinct religious sect, and in 1807 Universalists and Methodists were granted the same favor. Eventually, in 1819, the Young-Whipple Bill (known as the Tolerance Act) brought complete religious freedom to New Hampshire.

The Freewill Baptists of Wilmot, being in numerical superiority over other sects, were able to successfully postpone the completion of a Congregational church by moving the center of town activity far enough away from the building to prevent its acceptability as a meeting house. Much of the material for the first Baptist church (the present Methodist Church of Wilmot) was salvaged from the uncompleted Congregational structure.

The third church built in Wilmot was a Union church used by Calvinist Baptists, Universalists, Congregationalists and Freewill Baptists. When pews were sold to pay for a rebuilding after fire destroyed the old church, the Freewill Baptist majority gained the control which it has since retained.

The present structure is widely used as an example of small New England village Colonial church architecture.

St. Andrew's Episcopal Church

Hopkinton, New Hampshire

The oldest stone church of Georgian style in New England, St. Andrew's, built in 1827, has an Ashlar (stone) façade, granite walls and gable ends of wood sheathing. It is famous for the three remaining original windows of hand-rolled glass.

The present spire, designed by the famous church architect Ralph Adams Cram, was added in 1930 with the intent of bringing it into greater harmony with the Colonial style than the original flat-topped tower as designed by John Leach.

Originally called Christ Church, the name was changed to St. Andrew's when the present building was erected.

One of the early members of the congregation, Judge Matthew Harvey, governor of New Hampshire in 1830, had a family dog which habitually attended services at the church and lay quietly in the pew till the congregation was dismissed. The judge and his family, away for an extended period of time, left the dog with the Bailey family, who worshiped at the Congregational Church. The dog accompanied the Baileys each Sunday until they reached the Episcopal church, where he left them and went in and lay down in his master's pew till services were over. He then came out and waited for the Baileys to come by for the trip home.

The Unitarian Church of Concord

Concord, New Hampshire

This congregation was formed in 1827 when a group of young people withdrew from the First Congregational Church and formed the Second Congregational Society.

Their first visiting preacher advised the group to give up the effort to start a new church, but they persisted. They hired a hall and invited supplies to preach for them. One of the first preachers was a young Harvard Divinity School student who had not yet definitely decided to enter the ministry. He preached four times in December of 1827. During that time he met the girl he was to marry. The student preacher was Ralph Waldo Emerson. He and Ellen Tucker were married in 1829. She had been one of the first to sign the register of the Society and, before her marriage, she presented to the Society the beautiful silver Communion service used at the first Communion service in July of 1829—and used ever since. Tragically, Ellen's early death was the first recorded in the register.

The year 1959 saw the laying of the cornerstone of the building which now serves the congregation. It is a complex designed to have the appearance of a village, dominated by the free-standing spire.

The drawing was done from the loggia of the Carmelite Monastery across the road.

Carmelite Monastery

ROMAN CATHOLIC

Concord, New Hampshire

Here, in a small world apart, live nuns of the Order of Discalced (unshod) Carmelite Sisters of the Reform of St. Teresa of Avila. It is a cloistered Order which lives within the walls of a Papal enclosure, in complete and absolute withdrawal from the outside world.

The nuns are under the protection of the Holy See in Rome. They see no one from outside the monastery and only under extreme cause may Papal dispensation be sought or granted, which would allow departure from these walls. Though the sisters live apart from the world, they do not disregard it— theirs is a life of objective prayer for the world. They do not neglect civic duties. They register and vote by special absentee arrangements.

This Order lives on alms, which augment what they earn by their work in arts and handicrafts and the making of Church vestments. They raise much of their own food. They eat no meat; their diet consists of fruits and vegetables, fish, eggs and cheese.

Cause for the beatification of Mother Aloysius, the founder of this monastery, is now being prepared.

The only physical aspect of the monastery which can be shared by the sisters and outsiders is the interior of the chapel. Its stained-glass windows are extraordinarily fine. One long window, inside the loggia, shows the Apostles' Creed in words and symbology. It seems appropriate to use for illustration the first panel of that window as it can be seen by the sisters and visitors alike.

Quaker Meeting House

SOCIETY OF FRIENDS

Unity, New Hampshire

Remote from neighboring habitation, in the mountains of New Hampshire, stands this simple, unpainted structure, its clapboarding curled and colored to a rich brown patina by exposure to 144 years of wind and weather.

The adjoining horse shed is succumbing to the disintegration of neglect, but the moss on what remains of its roof gives silent testimony to the marriage of nature and structure. The old, square, hand-made nails are loose in their wooden beds, the line of the roof is no longer straight, the grass is yellow and tall, and everything seems exactly as it should be.

Through the windows can be seen the benches, standing neat in their rows. The separator panel, which can be dropped to make two rooms of one, is lifted, leaving a broad aisle down the middle of the room.

Just as austerity reflects coldness and deprivation, here utter simplicity reflects warmth, peace and sufficiency, a spiritual sufficiency which has no need of false reassurances or superficial embellishments.

What we have come to regard as the necessities of civilization and the amenities of sophisticated urbanity are absent here. It is as well that they are, for they would be intrusive redundancy.

The sign over the door states: "Quaker Meeting House Built by that Society in 1820." As it was built then it is used now.

Bethany Covenant Church

EVANGELICAL COVENANT CHURCH OF AMERICA

Manchester, New Hampshire

The human need to identify with a group—to feel at home, to speak a common language, to share familiar customs—was responsible for the building of many churches throughout New England and America. Mill towns and cities had work to offer and attracted many people newly come to the land of freedom and promise. Manchester is such a town. Its many churches can be viewed as a chronology of immigration. Bethany Covenant Church is an important part of that chronology.

The Evangelical Covenant Church is a Christian denomination which has its roots in Sweden. The Swedish immigrants who settled in this area seventy-five years ago, having no facilities of their own, worshiped for a time with Congregationalists. Lack of familiarity with the English language and a desire to follow their own faith sharpened the need for a Swedish church. The Congregational Church provided material assistance to the extent of financial subsidy to fill that need.

The first name of the Swedish church was "Svenska Evangeliska Missions Forsamling." It was later called Bethany Congregational, and ten years ago the present name was adopted.

It has been more than twenty years since services have been conducted in the Swedish language, and Bethany Church membership is now composed of multiple ethnic backgrounds. Even so, Bethany is commonly referred to as the "Swede's Church." Assimilation, acceptance and time have destroyed many of the prejudices which created stigmatic references and such names now serve only for ready identification—without derogatory intent.

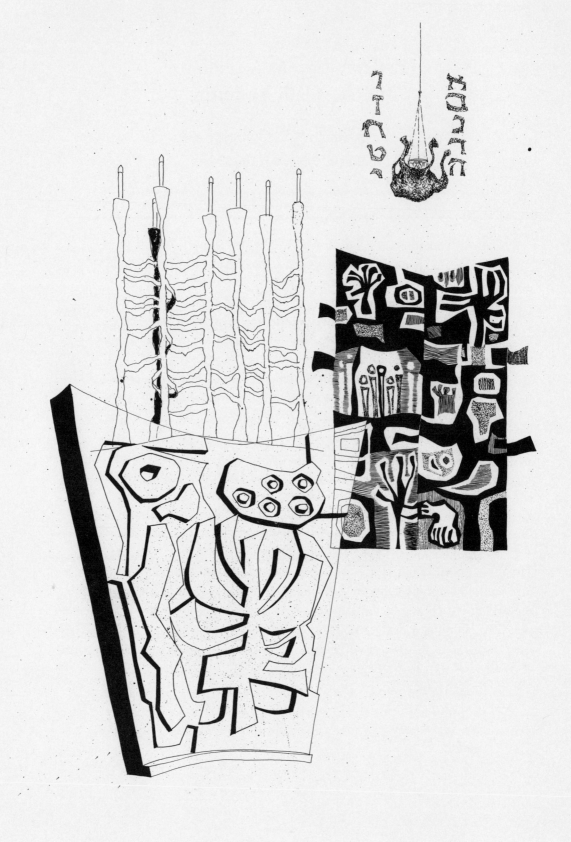

Temple Adath Yeshurun

JUDAIC REFORMED

Manchester, New Hampshire

From the temple dedication of 1959 (5719), the following is a part of the message from the rabbi of the congregation:

Life is dynamic. It is forever changing. Institutions fall under the same law of change as human beings—as all life does. Although on the surface a building appears to be no more than mortar and brick, yet, so long as buildings represent human life, these too come under the law of mutability.

Much has changed in congregation Adath Yeshurun in the half century of its existence. It has grown and has outgrown its physical facilities. Through devotion, sacrifice and generosity it has provided new, magnificent facilities for worship and study. Spiritually, too, it has moved forward. Finding some ancient customs, prayers and traditions lacking in meaning for our age it has introduced new customs, different prayers, a more acceptable interpretation of Judaism.

All this has come about as a consequence of the law of growth, and a passionate desire on the part of our constituency to preserve the great teachings of Judaism.

Adath Yeshurun has kept pace with the times and made every compelling adjustment. During the years, it has BROKEN DOWN whatever became a hindrance to its progress and it has BUILT UP whatever was useful and necessary to its life.

The montage drawing is a representation of the free-standing outside sculpture wall, the eternal light, the ark curtains and the Menorah, which exemplify the contemporariness of the spirit and the great art which beautify this temple. Dag Hammarskjöld's words on art exactly fit these works:

Art gives more to life than it takes from it. True art does not depend on the reality about which it tells, its message lies in the new reality which it creates, by the way in which it reflects experience.

First Unitarian Society

Milford, New Hampshire

The Milford Town Hall meeting room served this congregation as its place of worship from 1833 to 1870, when the Victorian-style stone church was built of Milford granite which was hauled from the quarry by oxen.

This is an excellent example of the architecture of a time when nothing was left simple or unadorned with curlicues.

To most viewers today, the sight of this structure will provide little esthetic pleasure or satisfaction, but to members of the congregation it is like a dearly beloved relative in whom only beauty can be seen. It is an honest statement and reflection of the time in which it was created. Certainly, this building does show solidity and craftsmanship of a type that is responsible for such clichés as "they don't build them like that any more."

From the church calendar for October 25, 1964, the following words seem particularly fitting:

The members of this society welcome all who worship with us this morning. This is a church from which no man can be excommunicated . . . but by the death of goodness in his own breast.

Holy Trinity Cathedral

NATIONAL CATHOLIC CHURCH

Manchester, New Hampshire

Sixty-eight years ago, a Polish-American Roman Catholic priest, the Rev. Francis Hodur, founded the Polish National Catholic Church in Pennsylvania.

At that time there was considerable resentment felt by many of the Polish immigrants against the Roman Catholic Church because they had no voice in the selection of their parish priests. The fiercely independent nature of a people too-often subjugated manifested itself in this case in a religious rebellion. Such an action is the more remarkable when viewed against the background of piety and devotion which is characteristic of the Poles.

Now this denomination, which has its closest ties with the Anglican Church, has spread to all parts of the United States, to Canada and to Poland itself.

Its several differences from the Roman Church are similar to those of the Anglican and Ukrainian churches, with services conducted in the mother tongues of the congregations.

The architecture of the church is Romanesque, with domes rather than spires capping the towers. The Slavic heritage of the church's people is evidenced by its colorful interior.

St. George Hellenic Orthodox Church

Manchester, New Hampshire

The turn of the century saw the arrival in Manchester of a Greek community which almost immediately built its church, a building which is coming to the end of its service as a place of Greek Orthodox worship.

Greco-Americans have always maintained close ethnic ties, but even the tightest of such relationships must give way to the influences which divorce young people from old concepts and parental memories. The successes of the fathers and grandfathers in building new lives with enlarged opportunities for their children have themselves contributed most importantly to the need for a new church and center which will keep alive Greek customs and traditions in Manchester.

The new St. George's will be a neo-Byzantine combination of traditional forms evolved and stated in contemporary terms. Its complex of facilities will include church, community center and twelve classrooms to be used by the Sunday school and the regular afternoon Greek school.

Orthodoxy and the Greek heritage will continue to be handed down to the new generations despite the expiration of the tight-knit neighborhood which is dying a natural death as the young Greco-Americans achieve fuller assimilation and integration with their countrymen.

St. Mary's Ukrainian Catholic Church

Manchester, New Hampshire

Manchester offers a singular opportunity to see what has happened to "the huddled masses" who were welcomed by the Statue of Liberty. This mill and shoe-manufacturing city drew many ethnic groups—among them, Ukrainians, whose church, which uses the Julian calendar, is an offshoot of the Roman Catholic faith.

Ukrainian Catholics are under the jurisdiction of the Holy See in Rome but they have their own bishops and their own vestments, and the Ukrainian clergy are permitted to marry.

The lengthy services are conducted in Old Church Slavonic, with only choral music to accompany the liturgy. Leavened bread is used in the Communion of this faith, which requires the strictest fasting.

The sanctuary *(Ikonostas)* is enclosed and separated from the congregation by royal doors in the middle and deacon's doors on the sides. There is no statuary in the church, which is decorated by ikons. The altar is in the center of the sanctuary, away from the walls. The written language of the church employs the Cyrillic alphabet.

The exterior structures of the Ukrainian church are characterized by a traditional domed tower in place of a spire.

All Saints Parish

EPISCOPAL

Peterborough, New Hampshire

This must be considered one of the most beautiful of churches anywhere; there is a totality of beauty from setting to architecture to windows to furnishings and accouterments. Of it, Amy Coburn Lyseth wrote in the *American Magazine of Art:*

Here in Peterborough seems transplanted an ancient English rural church, but with a difference. Under the hands of the skillful architect, Ralph Adams Cram, the awkwardnesses of medieval builders have been avoided. In All Saints there is light and spaciousness, movement and life although the style, Transitional Gothic, is always felt. The unity throughout, even in the color of the furnishings, is too consistent and elegant for a veteran of the mother-countries that has weathered the vicissitudes of a thousand years, the despoiling and arbitrary re-modeling of successive generations. . . .

Of one of the stained-glass windows she writes:

Composed of graceful mosaics in close, small pieces of ruby, blue and silver, it calls to mind those in Chartres and Bruges, seldom emulated on this side of the Atlantic.

Like the churches of old, it is built of local materials, the warm-colored granite having been quarried on the immediate property. The quarry was opened for this one purpose and closed on its completion. The structure is built according to medieval construction principles and methods. It was con-structed to last for centuries as a true shrine and a thing of and for the community it serves.

Cathedral of the Pines

INTERFAITH ALTAR OF THE NATION

Rindge, New Hampshire

In a needle-carpeted pine grove on a hill overlooking Mt. Monadnock is located a remarkable place of worship.

On this exact spot, Sanderson Sloane had decided to build his home. He did not live to fulfill that dream. As Lieutenant Sloane, he was killed over Coblenz in 1944. In his memory, Sloane's parents created this tribute dedicated to Almighty God as a memorial for all American war dead, military and civilian—recalling especially the debt we owe the Creator of those lives.

Cathedral of the Pines is an International Shrine. The Congress of the United States unanimously voted recognition of it as the Altar of the Nation, though national or state authorities have no jurisdiction here, *per se*, nor has any church or member of the clergy except at the time of his service. All religious faiths are welcome to use the Cathedral and almost fifty different faiths have held services here.

Built into the walls of the small hilltop house are gifts which have come from all areas of the world. A piece of the Blarney Stone, a Viking axe, a fragment of the Sepulchre of our Lord, a stone from Auschwitz—the list would be almost endless. The building houses an altar and an ancient Spanish Ark of the Covenant.

From its creation as a personal memorial the Cathedral has developed, entirely through voluntary contributions, into a trust administered by a board of trustees composed of outstanding lay people of different faiths and origins.

Conceived and created in parental love, flourishing in brotherly love, the Cathedral today is a heartening assurance of the oneness of mankind where the intent of the founders to obey the command "Thou shalt love the Lord thy God and thy neighbor as thyself," and our Pledge of Allegiance—"One nation, under God, *indivisible*"—gives promise that the tranquil light of peace may shine on these pines.

VERMONT

Vermont—freedom and unity

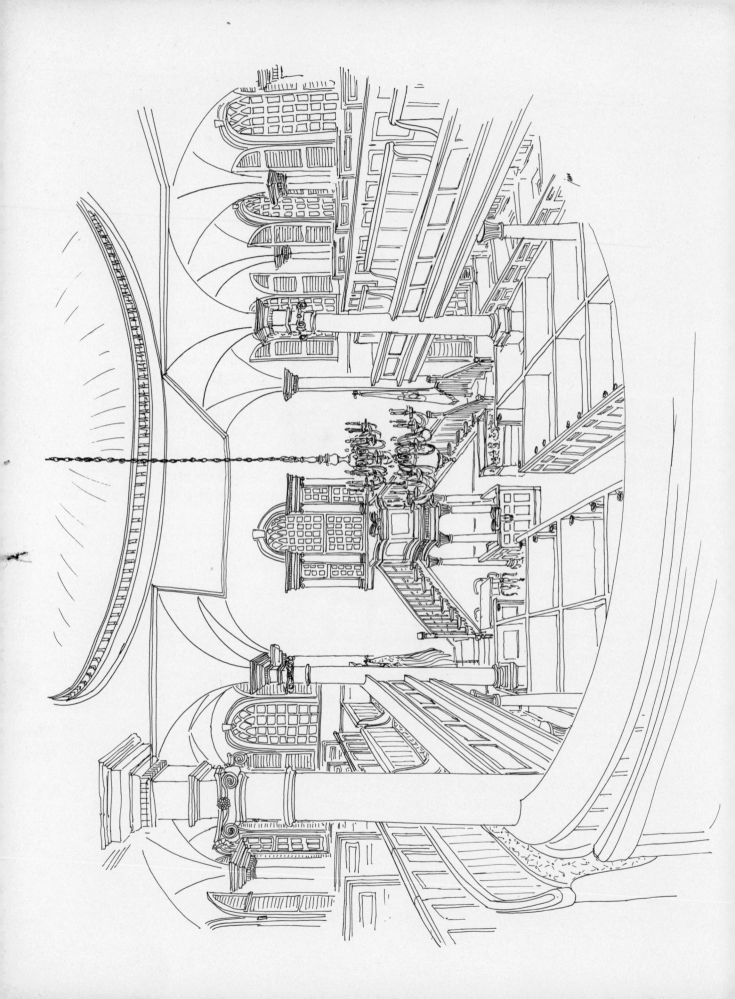

Old First Church

CONGREGATIONAL

Old Bennington, Vermont

Bennington was the first settlement in Vermont and the First Church is the state's oldest, as is the adjacent burying ground, whose first occupant was the Widow Harwood. This good lady was part of the first group of twenty-one pioneers who settled here. As the group approached the town site the women organized a race, which was won by Widow Harwood. Seventeen months later she died—while plowing her fields. The same horse which first bore her across the town line and pulled her plow bore her to her grave.

It was in the old meeting house that, for eight successive sessions, the legislature of the fiercely independent Republic of Vermont sat to make its laws. (Vermont was an entirely independent republic till its admission into the Union on March 4, 1791.)

It was from Bennington that Ethan Allen led his Green Mountain Boys down the hill to stand against the incursions of the York Staters, who were trying to annex Vermont.

Here was fought the Battle of Bennington, which began the downfall of Burgoyne in the Revolution.

Restored to its colonial beauty, complete in every detail from box pews with their pewter candle holders to the fan light over the main entrance, with funds contributed by people from the entire state, this church and burying ground have been made Vermont's Colonial Shrine.

At the dedication of the restored church in 1937, Robert Frost read one of his poems, from which the following lines are taken:

> Most of the change we think we see in life
> Is due to truths being in and out of favour.
> As I sit here, and oftentimes, I wish
> I could be monarch of a desert land
> I could devote and dedicate forever
> To the truths we keep coming back and back to.

The Congregational Church

Middlebury, Vermont

The architect of this church was Lavius Fillmore, a cousin of President Millard Fillmore. For his basic designs for this and the Old Bennington Church, he used the Asher Benjamin book *The Country Builder's Assistant*. Construction began in 1806 and was completed in 1809. During those years the Vermont legislature met twice in the building.

In the hurricane of 1950, a falling tree, planted in 1839 by the first pastor, barely missed the corner of the building.

The church served as the College chapel until the nineteen-hundreds, with boys seated on one side of the gallery and girls on the other. Commencements were held in the church till 1939.

Philip Battell began the observance of Forefathers Day on December 21, 1842, in honor of the Pilgrims. The observance has been maintained as an annual event in this church, with the basic format unchanged; an important address in late afternoon or early evening, followed by dinner.

The only change from the original order was made in 1853 when the dinner, which had been strictly stag at the local tavern, brought the ladies into participation and the dinner to the church premises. The women cooked the food in their own homes and then took it, along with china, silver and napery, to the church, where each hostess served a table of twelve. One of the less affluent ladies who had no carriage or other conveyance simply loaded everything into her large baby carriage and trundled it to the church.

Today, most of the cooking is done in the church kitchens, but everything else remains the same.

First Congregational Church

Newfane, Vermont

The first meetings of the congregation at Newfane sat as a group called "The Liberal and Charitable Christian Society of Newfane." This was in the days when the town was located on the hill. When Newfane moved to the valley, both the church and the courthouse were moved bodily to the present site.

It was in Newfane that an unusual marriage ceremony was performed. A widow whose husband had left considerable debts wished to remarry, but neither she nor her prospective groom wanted responsibility for those debts— a liability the groom would, under the custom of the time, have normally acquired with the taking of a widow as his bride. The bride in this case went into a closet into whose door a small hole had been cut. She stripped herself naked, put her arm through the hole in the door, and was thus married. A maid gave her a new outfit of clothing provided by her new husband who, since he had received her in marriage with nothing inherited from his predecessor, was deemed not to have acquired responsibility for his debts.

Newfane was a strong center of Abolitionist sympathy and activity. Its sympathies for the Negro did not cease with the Civil War. In 1870 several young men of Newfane moved to and settled in Coushatta, in Red River Parish, Louisiana, where, as friends of the freedmen, they prospered in business and politics.

In 1874, on the night of August 27, they were roused by a noisy, threatening mob. To allay the tempers of the crowd they surrendered themselves, unarmed, in the belief that they were to be moved to Shreveport for safety. Three nights later they set out, under an armed guard of thirty men, but were met by another group. Abandoned by their "protectors," they were murdered. Their bodies were withheld from relatives till decomposition had removed evidence of the abuses they had suffered.

St. James

EPISCOPAL

Arlington, Vermont

As Bethel Church, organized in 1764, St. James was the birthplace of the Episcopal Church in Vermont. Until 1772 it was served by Captain Jehiel Hawley, a lay preacher.

The year 1837 brought the change of name from Bethel Church to St. James.

When the original church was extensively damaged by fire in 1829, the present building was constructed. The oldest "pure Gothic" structure in Vermont, built of gray granite and wood, its quiet dignity dominates the placid main street of Arlington. The neighboring burying ground is a pervasive reminder that the transience of man's life is tied to the permanence of his faith. Stone and wood combine in church and graveyard as subtle symbols of constancy and change brought together in natural harmony.

Arlington was so named in honor of Lord Arlington, Benning Wentworth, Governor of the Province of New Hampshire, who was commissioned by King George to charter the town on July 26, 1761. From Lord Arlington's name it is easy to fix the inspiration for the name of the older town of Bennington.

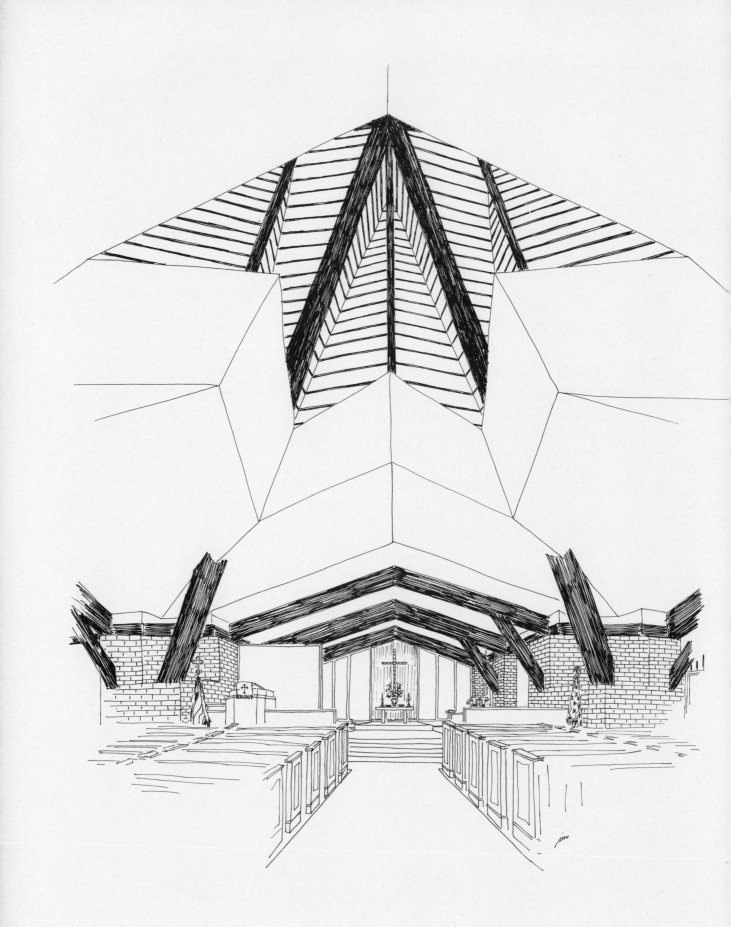

Second Congregational Church

Bennington, Vermont

In 1824 a small group of the Old Bennington First Church members, who felt that there should be a Congregational church more conveniently located in the town, began their efforts to accomplish this end.

There were those of the old church who felt that Bennington could not support two congregations, but the persistence of those who sought separation prevailed and the new church was gathered.

The history of this church is a testament to the tenacity and determination which enable men to overcome all kinds of adversity. From the start financial problems beset the congregation, and in 1864 its members were severely tried when the church was totally destroyed by a fire which was thought to have been the work of an incendiary.

Paradoxically, this congregation prospered during the difficult post-Civil War years of economic depression, and a new church edifice was planned and built. Then in 1874, the not-yet-completed 165-foot steeple was blown down and destroyed by gale winds and had to be totally rebuilt.

In 1958 work was begun on a new church, in which the first service was held on Christmas Eve of 1959. But the history of tribulations was not yet complete, for in August of 1961 the church sanctuary was ripped by a gas explosion. Reconstruction of the sanctuary was completed in time for services to be held again on Christmas Eve of the same year.

The four-pointed star design which forms the fifty-foot tower is carried by extension to develop the cruciform floor plan of a building which is a memorial to the endurance of one congregation's faith in its church and itself.

Union Christian Church

NONDENOMINATIONAL

Plymouth, Vermont

Nestled in a tight little valley of the Green Mountains of Vermont is the tiny village of Plymouth, where Calvin Coolidge, our thirtieth President, was born, lived and worshiped in the simple structure located behind his birthplace and across the narrow road from his home. The church is as simple and spare as was Calvin Coolidge himself.

In the small chapel, finished in natural wood, the late President worshiped by the light of a kerosene lamp candelabrum. The coldest winter months of Vermont were severe enough that even the vigorous natives found the unheated church uncomfortable. At such times services were held in the Coolidge parlor.

Inside the entry of the church is displayed a marble tablet on which is carved the following quotation from a Coolidge speech delivered at Bennington, September 21, 1928.

Vermont is a state I love.

I could not look upon the peaks of Ascutney, Killington, Mansfield and Equinox without being moved in a way that no other scene could move me.

It was here that I first saw the light of day; here that I received my bride; here my dead lie pillowed on the loving breast of our everlasting hills.

I love Vermont because of her hills and valleys, her scenery and invigorating climate, but most of all, because of her indomitable people. They are a race of pioneers who have almost beggared themselves to serve others. If the spirit of liberty should vanish in other parts of the union and support of our institutions should languish, it could all be replenished from the generous store held by the people of this brave little state of Vermont.

Our Lady of Mercy

ROMAN CATHOLIC

Putney, Vermont

The histories of Putney's churches are interwoven in a harmonious pattern. The Methodist, Baptist and Congregational faithful are presently served by one United Church. The old Baptist Church building is now used as the Town Community Center, and Our Lady of Mercy was formerly the Methodist Church.

Across Main Street from the Catholic church stands the small residence that once was the chapel of Putney's contribution to the list of human religious faiths. In 1834, John Humphrey Noyes, an ordained Congregational minister, rebelled against the tenets of that church when he adopted "Perfectionism," a belief that held that Christ had completed his work of saving man from sin.

Noyes' license to preach was withdrawn and he was excommunicated from the Congregational Church. He then went on to develop a system which he called "Bible Communism," whose unconventional society was tolerated by the Putney community until it was learned that the principles of the faith permitted its members to share wives as well as earthly possessions and called for renunciation of allegiance to the United States.

As the head of the "Free-lovers," Noyes was arrested, but he fled to New York before he could be tried. He was joined by a hundred and fifty of his followers and set up the Oneida Community, which in 1879 abandoned the practice of complex or promiscuous marriage. This action cost them their leader.

Putney is the home of the Experiment in International Living, Windham College, and a fine private school.

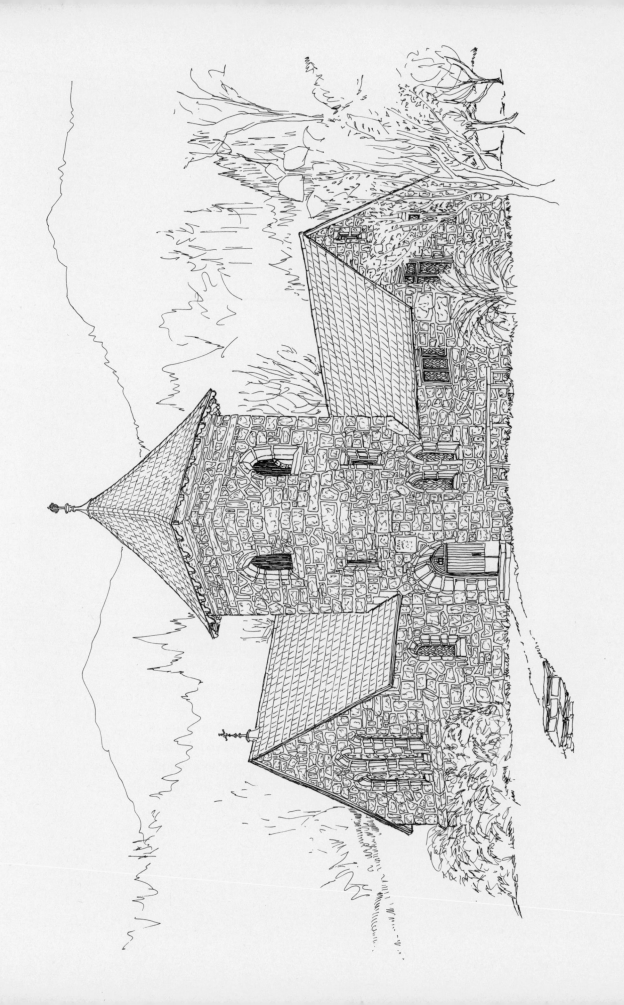

Mission Church of Our Saviour

EPISCOPAL

Killington, Vermont

For the sum of one pound, one shilling and sixpence, Josiah Wood, in 1798, purchased the Whole Right of Land to about 336 acres at the foot of Mount Killington, and there built his house.

On the site of this house, one of his children, Elizabeth, born in 1804, was ninety years later to build the Mission Church, dedicated to the ten children of Josiah and Judith Wood.

The church is built of white granite from the neighboring hills, in the style of English churches. The sanctuary lamp was designed and made at the Mission, as was the cross of the beautiful hanging rood, carved from oak cut on the property. The Corpus was carved in Oberammergau by Anton Hoser.

A Mission church is a dependent—a child of the diocese whose bishop is rector of the Mission. The incumbent priest is the vicar, or priest-in-charge. At Killington, the vicar has responsibilities which go beyond normal ecclesiastical duties. He keeps alive the traditional relationship of this church with nature, for he is farmer, orchardman, husbandman and host as well as priest.

At this Mission is found the warmth of genuine hospitality in a home spiced with the smell of fruits being preserved; a home alive with the sound of children's play, humble with a simple religiosity, rich with love of man, solid with the toil of the land, blessed with happiness.

Blessed Sacrament Church

(Brother Dutton Memorial)

ROMAN CATHOLIC

Stowe, Vermont

This rustic chapel of natural pine was dedicated in 1949 by the bishop of Burlington. It serves the Stowe Catholics and the skiers who throng here in the winter months.

The unusual exterior decor is a memorial to the Stowe-born Joseph Dutton, a converted Catholic who for forty-four years devoted his life to the lepers at the colony on the island of Molokai, where he died at the age of eighty-eight.

Dutton, after noteworthy service in the Civil War and an unsuccessful marriage, took to drink and became something less than a model of respectability.

Another metamorphosis took Dutton out of a wasteful life into the Catholic Church and a two-year residence in a Trappist Monastery. On his departure from the monastic life he read of the work of Father Damien at Molokai, and Dutton determined that the rest of his life would be devoted to this good work.

Dutton made his way to Molokai, never to leave it. For three years he assisted Father Damien, until the death of that benevolent man left him in charge of the work which was to be his responsibility for the next forty-one years. He never accepted a penny of recompense for his services. Because of his good works the title Brother was conferred on him by popular acclaim and he was thenceforth known as Brother Joseph.

In 1908, President Roosevelt rerouted a fleet of sixteen battleships so that they might pass the leper colony in battle formation, flags dipped, in salute to Brother Joseph and his lepers.

On the outside walls of the church, the French artist André Girard painted scenes from the lives of Father Damien and Brother Joseph with the lepers.

Quaker Meeting House

AMERICAN SOCIETY OF FRIENDS

Burlington, Vermont

This simple building, unconverted, was once the stable and carriage house of the residence at 179 North Prospect Street, in Burlington. The present resident, a member of the meeting, is Professor T. D. Seymour Bassett of the University of Vermont.

The humble history of the meeting house, which is set in a small orchard, is appropriate to the essential humility and simplicity of Quaker worship.

The interior is no more elaborate than the exterior. Seating is on simple, wooden folding chairs set up in the circular arrangement typical of the newer college-town meetings. No longer is the group divided by sexes for the business meetings. No room divider exists in this meeting house. Such division was observed in early Quaker days, not as a form of segregation or denial of the equality of the sexes, but as a recognition that women would feel freer to express themselves if they were separated from the traditional domination of business affairs by the men.

The membership of the Burlington meeting is made up, in its major numbers, of people who have adopted Quakerism as their religion, having formerly followed other Christian or non-Christian faiths. The present growth of Quakerism, despite a notable lack of missionizing, seems to indicate an unusual fulfillment of contemporary religious needs by this faith.

The Burlington meeting's service activities are primarily local, such as the project of clean-up and improvement of blighted residential areas through weekend work camps directed by young Friends.

Church of Jesus Christ of Latter Day Saints
(Memorial to the Prophet Joseph Smith)

Sharon, Vermont

Sharon is the birthplace of the Mormon prophet Joseph Smith. Here stand the memorial shaft of Vermont granite and the chapel, the first Mormon church in Vermont. The memorial is thirty-eight and one half feet tall, to commemorate the thirty-eight and one half years of the martyred prophet's life. It is the world's tallest single shaft of granite.

Joseph Smith founded the Mormon faith in Palmyra, New York, after he had experienced a series of revelatory visions and had been shown the hiding place of the golden book of Mormon by the Angel Moroni, who also gave him the power to decipher the book from the ancient Egyptian hieroglyphics in which it had been written fourteen centuries earlier. It was a history of the civilization which, it said, had been brought from the Middle East to exist in this hemisphere from 600 B.C. to 400 A.D.

It was Joseph Smith's belief that there was to be a new Holy Land in the area of Independence, Kansas. He took his band of followers there in an unsuccessful effort to acquire land holdings for the Mormon faith.

The next stop in the movement of the Mormon flock was Nauvoo, Illinois, where the prophet taught. The persecutions which had been Smith's lot from the time of his visions followed to Nauvoo and, in nearby Carthage, he died a martyr's death at the jail, in the fury of a mob.

The prophet's disciples took the Mormons on their modern-day exodus to the Great Salt Lake, from whence the faith has grown and spread to include more than 2,000,000 members around the world.

MAINE

Dirigo

I guide

MAINE

Dirigo

I guide

The First Congregational Church

Kittery Point, Maine

Records show that there was a church at Kittery in 1659, but the Congregational parish was organized in 1714. The present meeting house was built in 1730. The beautiful pulpit is the original one, built for the church in the same year. Only two of the old box pews remain; one houses the organ and the other is that which was occupied by the Pepperrell family.

Sir William Pepperrell, said to have been the wealthiest man of New England, was one of the founders of the church. Sir William had been made a baronet by King George II for having won the siege of Fort Louisbourg on Cape Breton Island. It was the first large-scale, concerted military action by the English Colonies in North America.

The silver baptismal bowl still used by the church was given by Sir William. From this bowl, in 1730, the first child to be baptized in this church was William Whipple. He was to be one of the signers of the Declaration of Independence.

At the end of the Revolution, much of the Pepperrell estate was confiscated as Tory property, the baronet's grandson and family having earlier departed for England not to return.

The Lady Pepperrell Mansion, across from the church, was built in 1759. It is now owned by the Society for the Preservation of New England Antiquities and is a famous showplace.

The church parsonage is the oldest still standing in Maine. It was built in 1729 and contains many of the treasures accumulated through the two hundred and thirty-six years of its existence.

The First Church

Kennebunk, Maine

Stories attached to this one-time Congregational church point out, better than dry history, two now-vanished aspects of colonial religion.

Long sermons and intense cold in the unheated church led to the following colloquy between the minister and his wife. The minister asked his wife to make him some moccasins to keep his feet warm in the pulpit. Without hesitation she answered: "I won't do it. You preach so long now that you tire all the people out, and if you get a pair of moccasins it will be worse still. When your feet get cold you ought to leave off."

An itinerant preacher, Joseph Smith, in a haranguing sermon, said that the Congregational doctrines were the work of the devil. Knowing what Samson had been enabled to do with the Lord's help in pulling down the main pillars of the Temple, he said that he could, with the same Divine help, pull down this church. This he promised to do, naming day and hour for the deed. At the stated time Smith and his followers arrived to join the large crowd assembled to witness the promised destruction. After much prayer the preacher confidently grasped the sill and heaved, but he proved to be less than Samson. Repeatedly he prayed and strained to no avail. At last, one bystander yelled: "Better hoist it at the north end, Brother. Once you get that end up, the weight of the steeple will tip it."

The indignity of failure sent the minister from those parts, not to be seen there again.

Gustav Adolph Lutheran Church

SWEDISH EVANGELICAL LUTHERAN

New Sweden, Maine

The town of New Sweden was born in the mind of a Maine American, the Hon. William Thomas, Jr., while he served the administration of Abraham Lincoln as war consul to Sweden. When he returned to Maine he told the legislature of his plan to set up, in Maine, a colony of immigrants to be selected in Sweden. The plan was accepted and Thomas was appointed Commissioner of Immigration. He went back to Sweden and gathered a group of people he thought would make the best citizens. They set sail in July of 1870 and landed at Halifax. By wagon, the fifty-one settlers made their way to the then heavily forested wilderness that was to become New Sweden.

The Board of Immigration had cut out a rough woods road and had intended to raise twenty-five log cabins as a welcome, but the colonists arrived earlier than anticipated and only six cabins, one filled with supplies, greeted them. The next morning being Sunday, the first religious service was held—a sad occasion which marked the funeral services for a child who had died on the way.

By late September the Swedes had raised a two-story "Capitol." Downstairs were offices and supply rooms. Upstairs was the room used as church, schoolhouse and town hall. Today, this building is a museum.

The Lutheran congregation was formed in 1871. The church building was dedicated in 1880. Testimony to the prosperity and growth of the community and church is found in the existence of daughter churches at Stockholm and Caribou.

Celebrated annually at the church is the traditional Swedish Midsummer Eve Festival.

"Father" Thomas's *Mina Barn I Skogen* (My Children of the Woods) have proven the wisdom of his vision.

The Church of the Exaltation of the Holy Cross

ROMAN CATHOLIC

South Portland, Maine

The Roman Church was the first to bring Christianity to New England. The first church dedicated in what is now Maine was at St. Croix Island, near Eastport, in 1604, twenty-six years before the arrival of the Puritans. After St. Croix, a Mission was established at Mount Desert in 1613 and at Pentagoet in 1633.

A memorial window in the new Church of the Holy Cross commemorates the Indians and the Missions which made them the first Christians in New England.

Holy Cross's new building was dedicated in 1963. In its design tradition has given way to contemporary expression. The crowning glory of the exterior is the mosaic face of the slender tower, which portrays the life of Christ from the Nativity to the Resurrection. It is the only mosaic of its kind, formed of 350,000 pieces of Venetian glass.

Beautifully executed teakwood sculptures of Christ form the doors to the priests' cubicles of the confessionals. Over the confessionals are mosaics which display ancient Christian symbols. The rich warmth of the wood and the subtle colors of the mosaics provide a handsome contrast to the simple brick of the walls. It is a quiet emphasis of the importance of the confessional in the Roman Church.

Among the innovations of Holy Cross Church are a confessional specially equipped for the hard of hearing and the two mothers' rooms, glassed-in and sound-proofed, where parents of infants may participate in the Mass free from concern, knowing that their youngsters cannot disturb the congregation.

The Methodist Church

Houlton, Maine

The year of its incorporation as a town was the same year that brought a Methodist minister and church to Houlton. It was 1831.

For seven years services were held in the schoolhouse, until the Methodist minister and congregation were invited to share the Unitarian church, which was then without a minister of its own. It must have been a busy time for the Methodist preacher, who was serving a dual congregation and still had to maintain his work as a circuit rider, covering large areas to take religion to people who lived too far away to be otherwise served.

The year 1861 saw the building of the first Methodist church in Houlton. Thirty years later the growth of the congregation necessitated the erection of a larger structure to house the followers of the faith of John Wesley. This building stood for all too short a time. In May of 1902, Houlton was struck by a great fire which destroyed a large part of the town, including three of its churches. During the year that it took to build the present Methodist church, worship was shared with the Presbyterians, whose church had been spared the conflagration.

Methodism continues to flourish in Houlton. The church is at present at its largest numerical strength.

United Pentecostal Church

NAME PENTECOSTAL

Westfield, Maine

This church building which once served a Baptist congregation was, after the church had been vacant for some years, bought by the Name Pentecostalists, who have worshiped here since 1947.

The Pentecostal faith is based on the belief that Christianity began as a religion with the descent of the Holy Spirit on the Apostles on the seventh Sunday after Easter.

These are called "Name" Pentecostalists because they baptize in the name of Christ only. This is not a denial or lack of belief in God or the Holy Ghost. It is, rather, an emphasis of the belief that God is indivisible. That God was in Christ's body on earth. That Christ was God. That manifestations of God are not mere representatives of God but God Himself—and that because of the belief that Christ was God, baptism should be done in Christ's name alone.

The Pentecostalists feel a strong duty to carry their belief to the entire world. It is a faith of great depth and zeal whose emotional appeal has resulted in successful missionary work.

Located in the great, bare, wind-swept stretches of Aroostook County in upper Maine, this church seems to act as a reminder of the Pentecostal belief that God is everywhere.

Kingdom Hall of Jehovah's Witnesses

THE WATCHTOWER BIBLE AND TRACT SOCIETY

Caribou, Maine

Jehovah's Witnesses believe that there have always been Witnesses on earth, but in a purely organizational sense, the present movement was activated by Charles Taze Russell in 1879. The Society now has a membership of over 1,000,000, all of whom are active in its Bible education work. The Witnesses do not attempt to convert others, but they feel that a wider knowledge of the Bible will bring people closer to a true faith.

The Society is made up of congregations composed entirely of ministers, each of whom is charged with carrying the denomination's beliefs to the world in a door-to-door missionizing effort. They call themselves "Footstep Followers of Christ."

The twentieth verse of the twentieth chapter of the New Testament expresses the fundamental motivation of the Witnesses, all of whose activities are scripturally based:

. . . while I did not hold back from telling YOU any of the things that were profitable nor from teaching YOU publicly and from house to house.

Prayer, song and instruction are the three basic elements of the five services held weekly in the Kingdom Halls, which are the Witnesses' seats of worship. These services serve multiple purposes. They are as well organized and employ the same modern techniques as an efficient sales force.

The fundamentalist beliefs of the Witnesses subject them to ridicule and suspicion. There are those who find it difficult to accept or understand the Witnesses' proscription against transfusion or the introduction into the bloodstream of matter they consider foreign to an individual's natural blood. The Witnesses believe in the "Sanctity of Blood," and are more concerned with their everlasting lives than with their tenure on earth. They believe that the Bible contains all truth, which science must not contravene.

Drive-in Church—Rain or Shine

NONDENOMINATIONAL

Presque Isle, Maine

For many years in America a man's house and church were considered his two homes. That was before the automobile had put the country on wheels.

In recognition of the fact that greater mobility has increased recreational and diversionary activity, Bethany Baptist Church of Presque Isle has sponsored a drive-in church.

It was bound to happen: drive-in eating places, drive-in banks, drive-in supermarkets, drive-in telephone booths. Drive-in churches had to follow.

Services are held at eight o'clock on summer Sunday mornings —an early enough hour to permit a full, unbroken recreational day after worship.

Neither children nor adults have to dress up. It is a "come-as-you-are" informality which pipes the sermon into each car parked before a great blank screen that scant hours earlier had flashed Hollywood's messages to the Maine fields and mountains.

Attendance here and at Houlton, where another drive-in church is sponsored by the Military Street Baptist Church, has been good through the four years that this form of worship has been carried on.

It is a peculiar amalgam of civilization and nature which demonstrates an important facet of these times. In a day when all labors are being made easier for men and women, why should not religion, too, be made convenient?

First Parish Church Meeting House

UNITARIAN

Castine, Maine

Historic Castine, located at the tip of a peninsula in Penobscot Bay, is the only place in Maine to have existed under four flags—Dutch, French, British and American.

Castine's earliest non-Indian settlement was a French fishing station established in 1556. The Baron de Castin, after whom the town is named, came here in 1667 to live among the Indians. He married the daughter of the Sachem Madockawanda. His life and example made easier the work of converting the Indians to Catholicism.

Castine's meeting house was the scene of many civil and criminal trials. The most noted was that of Peol Susup, a Penobscot Indian tried for murder in 1817. The Sachem, Governor Neptune, made a successful plea in Susup's defense:

Rising with great dignity, Neptune stood for a moment with bowed head but with body erect; then, after looking above, and facing in turn the east and the other cardinal points, he commenced his plea:

"One God make us all. He make White Man and He make Indian. He make some White Man good and He make some Indian good. He make some White Man bad and He make some Indian bad. But one God make us all. Hope fills the hearts of us all. Peace is good. These, my Indians, love it well; they smile under its shade. The white man and the red man must always be friends. The Great Spirit is our Father. I speak what I feel."